JOYCE BROTHERS, Ph.D.

Better Than Ever

SIMON AND SCHUSTER
NEW YORK

Grateful acknowledgment is made to the Boston
Women's Health Book Collective, Inc., and Simon
& Schuster, Inc., for permission to reprint an ex-
cerpt from Our Bodies, Ourselves, copyright ©
1971, 1973.

Library of Congress Cataloging in Publication Data

Brothers, Joyce Diane.
    Better than ever.

    1. Women—Health and hygiene. 2. Middle
age—Health and hygiene. I. Title.
RA778.B876   613'.04'244   75-23380
ISBN 0-671-22173-6

To my loves—
my husband, Milton Brothers
my daughter, Lisa
my parents, Estelle and Morris Bauer
my sister, Elaine Goldsmith
my mother-in-law, Tillie Evans

Contents

CHAPTER ONE

Better Than Ever

One afternoon my daughter, Lisa, and I were going through our collection of family snapshots. There was one Milt had taken of me before we were married. I looked at that long-ago girl, smiling at the man she loved, and thought, "Oh, if I could only start all over again knowing what I know now. If only I had a second chance . . ." At that moment I was sorry I did not believe in reincarnation. It must be very comforting to feel that one has many more lives ahead in which to act upon the wisdom that it takes us so long to acquire.

That picture, taken over a quarter of a century ago, reminded me of that bitter quip about youth being too precious to waste on the young. It is right. It really is.

That evening I told Milt, "Don't laugh, but I think I started being middle-aged today. My butterfly years are over."

He did laugh.

"Forget it," he said. "Middle age is a thing of the past. Your butterfly years are still ahead. You are just emerging from your cocoon, dear. It takes a lot of living to produce a butterfly."

I smiled and said, "I hope you're right." It was just Milt's way of being reassuring, or so I thought, and of putting an end to the subject. (Men detest hearing women talk about getting older. It reminds them that they themselves are no longer 29.) I was not convinced, but I told myself that I had a wonderful husband, a wonderful daughter, a career that many women would envy. What more could a woman ask?

A woman *could* ask a lot more, I was to discover. And could have a lot more—if she wanted it. My husband was right. The great years, the prime time of a woman's life, are increasingly those after 40. Middle age is no longer a valid concept. Today women have that second chance that I was longing for, a chance to profit from all they have learned during those often difficult and strenuous "cocoon" years between 20 and 40. Now that women are having their children at a younger age and having fewer children, now that the social environment is more receptive to women playing vital roles in business and society, now that sex and age discrimination are gradually disappearing (sex discrimination faster than age), now that the menopause no longer means the end of a woman's youthful looks and vitality, now that a woman's average life expectancy at 40 is nearly 80—women have a second chance at life. A whole lifetime ahead of them at 40, a second chance to shape their lives.

I first became aware of this wonderful second chance women have through a rather upsetting experience that gave me the opportunity to see myself as I thought others saw me—and I didn't like what I saw. It was as traumatic as any adolescent's identity crisis; in fact, it *was* an identity crisis. Later, the experiences of other women opened my eyes to the really tremendous potential for growth and happiness that exists for women over 40 and made me realize how entwined our appearance and our self-esteem are—and how both work together to form a combination that unlocks the door to a woman's second-chance years.

This book tells how I went to work to lose weight, get my figure back to where it was when I was 20, and take a good ten years off my looks. How, in the course of this self-improvement program, I found a new personality emerging—happier, more relaxed, more competent. How my career branched out in fresh directions. How my husband began seeing me through more appreciative eyes. And how Milt and I recaptured the bliss and excitement that had marked the early years of our marriage.

I have outlined the practical steps any woman can take to look better, feel better and live better in that second lifetime that only women can truly enjoy. Not that anyone can achieve eternal youth—or should want to. But we can all take advantage of the scientific and psychological breakthroughs that enable women to embark on their second forty years with confidence and happy expectations.

Any woman who really wants this second chance can have it. But don't hesitate. Grab your chance. It is your life. And it should all be better than ever now.

CHAPTER TWO

She's *Not*
the Real Joyce Brothers

"She's scowling," said the man from the advertising agency.

"She's talking with her hands," said the public relations man.

"She doesn't look at the camera," said the director.

"She doesn't do anything for the clothes," said the marketing man.

There they were—the producer, the director, the president of the advertising agency, the vice-president of the advertising agency, the president of the division, the vice-president for marketing, some people I did not even know—all the brass.

And there I was.

We were in a small screening room. The lights were dimmed. We were watching television. To be precise, we were watching videotapes of the first three *Living Easy* shows. I was that "she" they were talking about.

This show meant a lot to the sponsors who had invested a million dollars in the new five-day-a-week program.

In a way, it meant even more to me than to the sponsors. I had been a television guest more often than I can remember, but this was my first real, big-budget, daily show of my own. I wanted it to be successful. I wanted it to be *terrific!* I had had my own daily radio program for years on which listeners called in to discuss their problems, but that was different. On radio, for instance, I often did not put on my makeup until the early morning show was over. Who would see me? Just the producer and the engineer. As long as I was clean and wide-awake that was all that mattered.

Television was something else again. That was what I was learning as the criticisms flowed on relentlessly—and impersonally.

"She's so stiff. Like a puppet."

"There's no bounce. The show lacks pace."

"And look at her legs!" someone said.

I looked at them on screen. There they were, neatly tucked under my chair. Knees together, ankles together. Very proper, and not at all bad. In fact, not bad at all.

"What's wrong with my legs?" I asked in outrage. I could take a lot of criticism, especially professional criticism. But my legs! "They are your best feature," my husband once told me. "That is, next to your logical mind." (What kind of compliment is that, anyway? Well, it's the kind I used to get from Milt.)

"What's wrong with my legs?" I asked again. "They look all right to me."

"Oh, your legs are all right," said the director, "but you aren't *using* them." For a moment I thought wildly, "Using them? What does he expect me to do? Juggle oranges with my feet while I'm interviewing? Peel potatoes with my toes?"

He went on, "You've got them stuck under the chair so it looks as if you're some kind of a freak sitting there. You've got to get them out front."

It was not the first time I had heard that criticism. Johnny Carson used to tease me on *The Tonight Show* by talking about the day they locked my knees together. I was always a little inhibited when I appeared on television, which resulted in my sitting bolt upright in my chair—my knees together and my hands folded in my lap like the best little girl in Sunday School.

"Let's have that sequence over again," the director said, "and Joyce, you watch your legs."

I watched. There I went. Across the stage to welcome my guest. Anthony Quinn was our big name that day. We both sat down, and just as I leaned forward and said, "Tell me, Mr. Quinn . . ." there they went. Those stupid feet seemed to scuttle underneath the chair all by themselves. To the camera, I was all knees. I sighed. It really did look dreadful.

"Now look," the director said, "here's how you should sit."

He got up, went to the front of the screening room, pulled out a chair and sank gracefully down like a model. His long, trousered legs slanted off to the side. His feet in their expensive Gucci moccasins were carefully pointed to lengthen the line of the legs and slim the ankles.

"See what I mean?" he asked. "Those are legs," he said with satisfaction. "You can do that, can't you?"

"Sure. I can do that," I said. And furtively, thankful for the darkened room, I inched my legs out from under my chair and slid them to the side, carefully pointing my toes.

We watched those first three *Living Easy* shows all the way through, then the lights were turned up and everybody started jumping on me in earnest. They reminded me of the flamenco dancers Milt and I had seen in Spain one summer. It was as if each one of my colleagues took a turn in jumping on me, banging his heels on me and telling me what was wrong. And they were so right.

I agreed with everything they pointed out to me. I could

see that I was not involving the audience at home in their living rooms. I was acting as if I were at home in my own living room having a serious conversation. I frowned when I got interested. I talked with my hands. I forgot to face the camera.

Everyone was surgically frank. There was no malice in it. They were professionals criticizing a professional performance. But I was sitting there absolutely horrified. Not only did I recognize that there was plenty of room for improvement in my performance; there was also plenty of room for improvement in my appearance.

I came across as a pleasant-looking, intelligent woman, but a little staid, a little flat, and much too serious. Was that the real Joyce Brothers? She was putting on weight.

Have you ever caught sight of your reflection in a store window or an unexpected mirror, and had a moment of shock? Who is that woman? That woman with her rear end sticking out? Her stomach sticking out? A roll of fat over her bra in the back?

Did you ever get a sudden glimpse of yourself and realize that you did not look young anymore? That you were no longer slim, but beginning to thicken through the middle?

That is what happened to me in the screening room. I saw myself from the back and the side, sitting and standing and walking. So that was the way others saw me.

It was not the way I saw myself. But then we never, never (or hardly ever) see ourselves as others see us. Neither men nor women, although there is a fascinating sex difference between the way men and women see themselves in a mirror.

When a man looks in the mirror, he sees Mr. America. He sees only the good things about himself. It is only on his most despondent days that he will notice the thinning hair, the spare tire, the sagging jawline. Even when he shaves, he does not see that ghastly ungroomed creature in the mirror, because he is concentrating on his beard.

But a woman—a woman has been trained ever since she was a little girl to look in the mirror, not to see what's right, but to check what's wrong. Women are inclined to see their flaws rather than their assets. A woman looks in the mirror and thinks, "I need more lipstick," or "My eyeliner is not on straight," or "I look tired today." Even the most beautiful women. Shortly after she had been crowned Miss U.S.A., a few years ago, I asked Amanda Jones how she felt about being so beautiful.

"Beautiful?" Amanda said. "I never think of myself as being beautiful. I've never even *felt* beautiful. The closest I've come to it," she said, "is that some days I think I look better than others."

She was absolutely convincing. This lovely young woman does not think of herself as the beauty she is. Most beautiful women are like Amanda. They look in the mirror and say, "Oh, my God! Look at those circles under my eyes!" or, horrified, "Is that a hair on my chin?"

There is another side to a woman's self-image, however, and that is the ability to fool ourselves. We try to cheat the mirror. I do it all the time. After I make up, I always put my best face forward when I check it in the mirror. I lift my chin a little, smile and turn my head to my most flattering angle. When I look in a full-length mirror, I invariably straighten up and stand tall, pull in my stomach, tighten my buttocks and twist my body just the slightest so I will look thinner.

But the world does not always see us at our best angles. This afternoon I was seeing myself as other people see me. And I did not like what I saw.

I am not trying to say that I looked absolutely dreadful.

I didn't. After all, if I had not been attractive, no one in this world would have considered building a television show around me—and the fact was that they had.

I looked pretty good for my age. *For my age.* Hateful phrase. To me, it meant those little wrinkles around my eyes. That little extra pudge around the middle. I was not really fat according to the standard height and weight charts. At five feet one, I weighed 128—just the upper limit. But medical researchers are discovering that these charts are usually far too generous in the poundage they allow. I should have weighed somewhere in the vicinity of 105 to 110 pounds.

None of these little flaws was news. I had been conscious of them all for a long time, but, "Face it, you can't be young forever," I would think as I examined the inevitable accompaniments of the years—those little crow's feet, that little droop here and sag there. I had to learn how to live with them. Certainly they were nothing to get upset about.

But they were. And I was. I had suddenly seen them from a fresh perspective. And I was not going to live with them.

I was going to bring back the *real* Joyce Brothers.

All the time these thoughts were scurrying around in my head, the criticisms were coming hot and heavy, but finally they dwindled off. The meeting was over. I thanked everyone for taking the time and effort to stage this helpful "show-and-tell" session, then went home—and cried. It had been a rotten afternoon.

CHAPTER THREE

The Morning After

The next morning I started to take stock of myself. And I was very humble. More than humble. I was at the bottom. And I was in the mood to take action. I never wanted to see myself again with the little roll of fat over my bra in the back and that prim and proper manner.

The reason for the staid personality I projected was easy to diagnose. All my professional life I had been a psychologist. Listening to other people's problems, concentrating on their situations, I had kept myself correctly and professionally in the background, whether I was on television or in the board room of a big company that had sought my advice. As a result, I had never learned to put myself forward and let the world know, "Here I am! Take a look. This is me. Joyce Brothers! And we're going to have fun!" I would never have dreamed of projecting such an image. What would the members of the American Psychological Association think? It was bad enough when trade papers like *Variety* called me the "show-biz psychologist."

That was going to have to change.

If I wanted to make this show a success, I was going to have to start sparkling. Previously when I had been on television, it had usually been in very controlled situations. On the *Merv Griffin Show* or the *Mike Douglas*

Show, my role tended to be that of the knowledgeable professional who just sat there and informed people. There was no moving around, very little spontaneity—just chock-full-of-facts chitchat with a few quips thrown in.

If a fortune-teller had forecast that I would one day be doing a belly dance on my own television show or learning how to juggle in public, I would have laughed in disbelief. But this morning, engaged in my rueful self-assessment, I would have given anything for just a little more show-biz razzle-dazzle. And a little stardust too, please.

I was going to have to learn more about my business. I remember one day I visited Shari Lewis, on the *"Hi, Mom"* set. She was talking to her little puppet, Lamb Chop. As I watched, I realized that the sound man shifted the overhead mike to the puppet when Lamb Chop "spoke." This experienced technician had been so caught up in the make-believe character that Shari had created that he actually felt Lamb Chop was talking and believed he had to move the mike to catch his voice. I wanted to be able to create that kind of magic.

And there was something else that had to be changed. My figure. I had to lose weight, shrink that waistline, shed those bulges. And while I was about it, I wanted to move more gracefully, act and look younger.

Caring about looking well may seem strange for a psychologist, and flies in the face of some of the thrust of women's liberation doctrine, but as a psychologist I have been impressed with the weight of so much research that is proving over and over again that in our culture, for both men and women, being attractive gives you an enormous help in relationships with others. According to recent studies, we all firmly believe that beautiful people have beautiful personalities. We may not be aware of our bias, but we consistently judge them to be more sensitive, kind, intelligent, interesting, sociable, and exciting than less attractive people.

And that belief isn't confined to young adults. It's shared by kindergartners, teachers, and most of the rest of the people in our society. In one study, four-to-six-year-olds were asked to select the classmates they liked most and least. They picked the most attractive children as their favorites. Their teachers did likewise, and considered the less attractive children more likely to be trouble-makers. When we grow up, for both men and women higher salary levels and greater advancement have a high correlation with pleasant looks, at all ages and in all fields.

If people treat you as if you were sensitive, intelligent, interesting, sociable, and exciting, that increases the probability that you are going to live up to their expectations and *be* that way. And to think better of yourself.

Maybe one day, knowing this, we can learn to judge people less superficially and help others to do so, but at this moment, those are the facts of life.

After years of giving advice to others, it was time to dish some out to myself. And one of my favorite bits of advice is to tell people to make a list when embarking on a new project or dealing with a problem. It helps break it down into segments that can be dealt with. Instead of a huge frightening Mount Everest, you simply have a pile of rocks that can be handled one or two at a time. If properly used, the list-making approach can help you reach almost any goal just by breaking down the approach to that goal into its basic components.

(Let me make it clear that these goals do not include such heart's desires as a chateau in France, a mad night of romance with Paul Newman or Omar Sharif, or your secret longing to be queen of England. Lists are to help you think through the realities and the possibilities and plan how to cope with them, not to fulfill romantic fantasies. If it is any consolation, it is a psychological fact that most romantic fantasies are most satisfying when unfulfilled. One of my favorites is being the star of an enormously successful Broadway musical and having all the critics go mad over my dancing . . . my singing . . . my acting . . . my wit . . . my charm . . . my beauty. Move over, Ethel Merman. And you, too, Julie Andrews. Back to Brooklyn, Barbra. Make way for Joyce, the star of stars! Quite a fantasy for a woman who does not know how to "use" her legs in front of the television camera. But I like it. Fantasies have their useful roles, but not on a list.)

I picked up a ruled yellow pad and started my list. It was easy. I knew what had to be done.

1. Lose weight. Twenty pounds to be specific. That was what our last Thanksgiving turkey had weighed, I realized with a shudder. I was carrying around the equivalent of that huge bird—gobble and all.

2. Get rid of that prim and proper image. It was time for me to prove that blondes really *are* more fun.

3. Look and act younger. That was important. In television, it is appearance that counts, not neatness. I'd never look 20 again, but how about 30? Well, how about 35? That was something to aim for.

All right. It was time for a change. And time to start. I could add to my list or change it later if necessary. And it would probably be necessary. There is something about making a change—just about any change in your life—that triggers other changes. And because of this ripple effect, lists tend to become outdated even before you have completed your projects.

The ripple effect is a graphic term for the dynamics of change. Think of a pebble dropped in a pond. The ripples start and push out and out and out. If you drop a boulder, you get waves. So when it comes to making changes, I usually suggest starting with a pebble rather than a boulder if one has the choice.

I made my choice. My first project was to lose those 20 pounds starting immediately. I thought it was a pebble, but it turned out to be more of a boulder.

CHAPTER FOUR

I Was Born Hungry

My mother told me I was born hungry and I have never had any reason to doubt her. As a skinny, jump-roping schoolgirl, I packed away meals that would have contented a truck driver. Nothing, absolutely nothing, impaired my appetite. One family story—fortunately it is a funny one now—concerns the time, a short while after Lisa was born, that I was terribly ill with acute septicemia. When my temperature shot up above 105 degrees one day, the doctors were terribly concerned. They called Milt and my parents, suggested they come to the hospital because it was impossible to forecast what was going to happen. They hinted at the worst. When my parents and husband arrived, there was the woman who was supposed to be at death's door propped up on her pillows—eating a steak. I was determined I would not die hungry.

It was not until my late thirties that the ounces started clinging. Eventually they became pounds and my weight crept up from 103 to 128. The amazing thing was that I was able to turn a blind eye to my more substantial silhouette for so long. I knew that I was buying larger dress sizes. I was up to a 12, but I just did not let myself think about it. For several years now I had been shopping carefully for clothes that hung just right to conceal my no-longer-slim waist. But things were going to be different. That middle was going to lose its bulge.

I had set my goal—20 pounds. The charts say that 104 is the ideal weight for a woman my height with a small frame and 112 for a woman with a medium frame. I decided to split the difference. It was not going to be easy. I knew that. Not only did I have the appetite of a lumberjack, I was a between-meals nibbler—a handful of pistachio nuts here, a piece of candy there, a small chunk of cheese and a cracker, a few spoonfuls of ice cream. I always kept the cookie jar full for Lisa, but I dipped into it more often than she did. I loved cream in my coffee and butter on everything. Above all, I loved sweets. A day without a dessert seemed incomplete.

As an about-to-be dieter, I could think of only one thing I had going for me. I did not drink. That was one source of calories I did not have to worry about. At dinner once or twice a month, I would have a glass of wine and that was it. Alcohol in any form made me sleepy and not much else. Whatever it does for other people, what it did for me was make me non-functional.

I had one other asset. Willpower. But as a psychologist I was aware that willpower was strongest and most effective when exercised in behalf of something one really wants. While I really wanted to lose weight, I did not really want to go on a diet. I would much have preferred to have someone wave a magic wand and make those pounds disappear. Presto! But I knew it did not work that way. There is only one way to lose weight and that is to eat less, eat a balanced diet and let the pounds melt away slowly. Being married to a physician, I was well aware of the dangers of crash/fad diets. They can be worse than the dangers of overweight. And women over 38 to 40 should avoid these diets like the plague.

Medical researchers have discovered that the freaky fad diets based on eliminating carbohydrates, for instance, or any other basic food category from one's diet can be extremely dangerous. The ensuing weight loss is not simply fat, as doctors used to believe, but tissue and muscle. The brain may be deprived. And that is not good. Our brains need their share of nutrients.

Most people do not realize that an unevenly balanced diet (and crash diets are *not* evenly balanced) can push a woman into a depression. To put it bluntly, dieting has literally driven some women crazy. One of the most common ways of reacting to depression is to console oneself by eating. That starts what is known as the "yo-yo syndrome." The dieter goes on a crash/fad diet and loses weight. Then she becomes depressed as time goes by because certain absolutely essential nutrients, vitamins and minerals are lacking in her diet; not only is her body operating at a deficit, but her brain is too, so her emotions and reactions begin to deviate from the normal. But the dieter does not understand that this is why she feels so emotionally down. She is so depressed that she finds it impossible to stay on her diet. Very soon, she has eaten her way back to her previous weight—or above it. The symptoms of depression usually disappear. But the woman is left with a residue of guilt because she went off her diet, and of frustration because she had worked hard and given up a lot of her favorite foods, and a lot of the satisfaction she found in food to lose weight—and it had all been in vain. This guilt and frustration don't go away. They may lie low, but the next time the woman gets up her energies to go on a diet—and fails, then guilt and frustration, combine to make her feel even more depressed than she did the first time. She begins to feel that she is a failure because she can't win the battle against overweight.

If a woman experiences this try-and-fail sequence over and over again, the symptoms of depression are more striking each time—and take longer to disappear. I have known classic cases of depression that have taken years (and thousands of dollars in fees to a therapist) to alleviate. Another by-product of crash/fad diets is fatigue, both physical and emotional, and that may intensify the depression. The sufferer has no energy left to combat the destructive lethargy that usually accompanies depression.

As it so often happens, very shortly after I had read the findings relating depression to crash diets, I saw a real-life example. One of my friends.

Nellie was 43, an editor on a national magazine. She had gone on a 500-calorie-a-day diet prescribed by one of the most publicized diet doctors in the city. He supplemented the 500 calories with a daily injection that was supposed to help her burn off the fat faster and more efficiently and at the same time keep her from feeling hungry.

It was extremely effective. Of course, one of the well-known effects of fasting is that after the first three days one loses most sensations of hunger. The 500-calorie regime could be likened to a fasting diet as far as that particular effect went. And Nellie did lose weight. The pounds melted away. She lost 30 pounds in two months and was within 5 pounds of her goal of a 35-pound weight loss when we had lunch together. She looked tired, somewhat drawn. The laugh lines at either side of her mouth had deepened. But as she nibbled on a breadstick and drank several glasses of iced tea, she said she felt fine, just a bit tired and that she didn't have much energy.

"I expect that will change," she said, "when I have lost this last five pounds, and go onto a maintenance diet."

I did not see Nellie for another six weeks, but when I

did, I was shocked. She had gained back almost all the weight she had lost, and she looked terrible. Her face was puffy. She had circles under her eyes. And she told me, "I'm terribly depressed. I feel like crying all the time. And even though I'm eating a lot, I just don't have any energy. It's all I can do to get myself up and dressed in the morning. I don't go anywhere or see anybody."

"What does your doctor say?" I asked curiously.

"Oh, he's furious with me. He says that if I won't stay on the diet, there's nothing he can do for me. He has stopped giving me the injections."

I nodded. I had heard of similar episodes. Diet doctors can prescribe weight-loss diets that are fast, but too often the dieter either quits before she has attained her goal or bounces back to her former weight very shortly after she has attained her goal. And when these women run into trouble, many diet doctors just write them off. They do not give the necessary psychological and medical support. There are, of course, many reputable, excellent doctors who specialize in obesity. I do not characterize these men and women as "diet doctors." The diet doctors are the ones who become fashionable for a season, or a few years, because of their presentation of a crash diet. Their medical credentials are usually acceptable, but to my mind, they are diet merchandisers not medical men and they have done more harm than good to their patients, especially the women of 38 to 40 and over who follow their regimens.

I told Nellie about the research that linked crash diets to depression and said, "The reason you're feeling so down might be simple malnutrition. Why don't you go to your regular doctor for a checkup?"

"He'd kill me!" she said, "if he knew I'd gone to Dr. XX!"

"No, he won't. And you know it," I told her. "Go see him. You don't want to go around feeling the way you do."

Nellie went to her doctor who had seen her through all the aches and pains and physical checkups she'd had for the last twenty years. He found that she was seriously anemic and that her body chemistry was out of whack. He sat her down, spelled out the facts of dieting for her, prescribed some vitamin and mineral supplements, and warned her against going on any more "instant" weight-loss diets.

He outlined a 1600-calorie-a-day diet for her, which is fairly generous for her height, five feet seven inches, and her weight, 140. At that point, 2300 calories would have represented a maintenance diet on which she would neither lose nor gain. On a 1600-calorie allowance, she would lose a pound every five days. Remember, it takes a 3500-calorie deficit to lose a pound, and Nellie would now have a daily 700-calorie deficit, which would add up to a pound in five days. The doctor told her that she was going to have to stick to it for the next three months and that eventually, when she got down to 125 pounds, she could stabilize her caloric intake at around 2100 or 2200 calories a day, and that they would work out an acceptable diet together when she reached her proper, healthy weight.

Nellie was fortunate. She was so scared by the reaction she had had to her crash/fad diet that she was willing to stay with her slow but rational prescribed eating pattern until she reached her goal. Some women are more emotionally vulnerable than Nellie. And for those women who may find themselves in a similar situation, it is often wise to seek a little supportive therapy as well as a medically approved eating pattern if feelings of depression do not disappear with a balanced menu.

Another reason why crash/fad diets are most inadvisable for the woman over 38 or 40 is because even as early as 30, there is a significant loss of skin elasticity. When weight is lost too fast, the skin cannot adjust to it the way it did at 21. In fact, it may never be able to adjust to a fast weight loss. The result will be wrinkles and drooping facial skin. A woman may look like a prune or kind of a weary blood-hound—depending on her facial structure—and who needs that? The only cure for these wrinkles and sags is plastic surgery; a very expensive price to pay, especially when the wrinkles might have been avoided by proper dieting.

(There are many instances when I think plastic surgery is an excellent idea and a good investment and I will discuss this in Chapter Eleven, but I have never felt right about spending money to remedy what could have easily been avoided by using good common sense in the first place.)

Then there are women who have always had a finely drawn face, usually with high cheekbones. If they lose weight too fast, it leaves their faces looking skeletal long before the bulges on their hips and thighs have even begun to melt away.

I have seen too many actresses and television personalities who have gone on crash/fad diets. They lost weight—and they lost their looks. Oh, they came across fine on the television screen, because the thinner you are on television, the better you look, and their haggard faces, their new wrinkles, sags and bags, were disguised with clever makeup tricks. But off-screen, they seemed to have aged by at least a decade.

The face is not all that suffers. A too-rapid loss may leave the dieter with unattractive crepey skin around the midriff. And no woman really looks sexy no matter how great her figure when her shape is slipcovered in prune skin.

Crash/fad diets also take their toll on hair and nails. Hair loses its bounce and glossiness. It may fall out. The ends may split. All sorts of unbeautiful things. Nails may soften or become brittle and break or split. Sometimes they even become discolored and misshapen. And do not for one minute believe that swigging down quarts of gelatin drinks or swallowing gelatin capsules will help. It won't hurt, but doctors have discovered that it won't help, either.

The crash/fad diets may also be medically dangerous for the woman over 38 to 40. Unless a woman has been instructed by her doctor to lose weight for medical reasons and is on a medically imposed and closely supervised regime, no woman over 38 should ever ever ever go on a crash/fad diet. It is one of the worst things you can do to yourself.

I knew all this. I knew there was no magic way to lose weight. No abracadabra that would whisk away the pounds. I was convinced of the long-term health and beauty benefits of slow weight loss. But I was not convinced that a diet could be easy or enjoyable—let alone bearable—and I was not sure that I could stay on a diet long enough to reach my goal of taking off 20 pounds unless I could find a way to minimize the deprivations and discomforts of dieting.

I've always found great pleasure in food. I love to cook. I love to eat. It was going to take all the willpower that I could summon up to convince myself I wanted to eat less.

That is the terrible trap of dieting. We want to reach the goal—but we don't want to take the trip. It is too difficult. Only a masochist could enjoy being on a diet, I thought. And I was no masochist. I revel in creature comforts. I like warm rooms, crackling logs in the fireplace, silky fabrics, soft pillows, cuddly robes.

Was losing weight worth giving up the cream in my coffee? Not to mention the whipped cream on my sundaes?

No! No! Never!

"There's got to be a way," I thought. "I'll ask Milt." The nice thing about being married to a doctor is that, while he is never supposed to treat his own family, he is always there to answer your questions. That evening after dinner—and I remember it well, it was the last time I ever had two helpings of chocolate mousse with whipped cream —I said, "I want to lose some weight. Have you got any suggestions for an easy way?"

"Well, for starters," he said, "you might try limiting yourself to one helping of dessert. But you don't need to lose weight. You look fine to me."

That is one of the lovely characteristics of husbands. A woman can turn gray, lose her figure, add a chin—and her husband still sees her as she was when he fell in love with her. When they say "love is blind," this must be what they mean. The reason for this charming blindness is that husbands stop looking at their wives the way they used to. When a man sees an old girl friend for the first time in twenty years, he thinks to himself, "How old she's grown." But he is not aware of how the same twenty years have affected his wife's appearance. First, because it has been a slow, day-by-day change, and, second, because he will not allow himself to be conscious of the change. This inner censor is what helps him overlook that second chin, the droopy bosom, or whatever.

This does not mean that it is not worthwhile looking your best for your husband. If you look absolutely smashing, that inner censor relaxes and lets your husband see you with freshly appreciative eyes. He will take a second look at you, a look on the reality level—and he will then be convinced that he was right all along. You look just as beautiful as you did on your wedding day, and somehow much, much more appealing.

"Well, just the same," I said, "I have to lose a few pounds." (I saw no point in mentioning the grand total of 20 pounds, which had assumed the form of a monster turkey in my mind's eye.) "What do you tell your patients when you want them to lose weight?" I persisted.

"I tell them to cut down. Cut down on fats, we all eat too much. Cut down on sweets. Cut out drinking. Cut down on amounts."

That really was not what I wanted to hear. It was too sensible. Milt was only telling me what I already knew. And I did not want to do it—to cut down, to deprive myself, even though after those two helpings of chocolate mousse it all seemed easier to contemplate. At that moment I could not imagine ever being hungry again.

But I was. Just before bedtime. I went to the kitchen for a snack and suddenly realized—no more snacks. "Stop it. You're on a diet. Or you should be. No more snacks for you." My willpower—or was it my conscience—won that round. I went to bed hungry.

CHAPTER FIVE

Applying the Pleasure Principle

I was determined to turn my diet into a pleasure, but I had no idea how this could be done. It was going to take ingenuity—I was sure of that. But I felt strongly about it. This was going to be a long-term project, and who wanted to be miserable and hungry for months on end? Not me. I already had one idea of how to introduce a little pleasure into my new life on a diet. I planned to assemble a "Diet Trousseau."

When a woman gets married, goes on vacation, takes a trip to Europe, or learns that she's going to meet her husband's childhood sweetheart, she usually buys something new to wear. I was embarking on a voyage just as meaningful as any of these, and I knew I would enjoy it more if I had the proper outfit. I gave it a great deal of thought and made a list of the things that were necessary for my new venture and the things that would make it more fun. It *was* fun. Obviously the answer to the problem of how to transform a diet from an exercise in masochism to an acceptable, even enjoyable way of life was to apply the pleasure principle to it. So I set out one day and bought my Diet Trousseau. And I recommend it to every woman who has to lose more than 5 or 6 pounds.

My personal Diet Trousseau consisted of:

1. A four-ounce glass
2. Bathroom scales
3. Food scale
4. A notebook
5. A calorie reference book
6. A measuring cup
7. A set of measuring spoons
8. Two Teflon frying pans
9. Ribbon, glue and polyurethane to cover my vitamin bottles
10. A china tray to hold my vitamin bottles
11. An electronic calculator

I added to this trousseau later, but all the essentials were right here, gathered on my first diet shopping spree. Some of them are rather idiosyncratic—like the ribbon and tray for my vitamin bottles—others are absolutely necessary. If you are counting pennies, the basic Diet Trousseau would consist of the following:

1. A postal scale—to weigh food
2. A bathroom scale—to weigh oneself
3. *Agriculture Handbook 8*—to look up calorie counts*
4. A notebook

Since every family kitchen is equipped with a measuring cup and measuring spoons, these four items are the only absolute essentials that the dieter should acquire. And don't make the mistake of thinking you can get along without them. Not if you have a weight-loss goal of more than a few pounds.

It is a basic psychological precept that rewards are a

---

* Send a check or money order for $2.85 to: Superintendent of Documents, Government Printing Office, North Capitol and G Streets, N.W., Washington, D.C. 20401.

more effective way of obtaining desired behavior than punishments. Unfortunately, a diet is presented to us as one long punishment. The dieter knows that the reason she is on a diet is that she was "bad." She ate too much. She gained weight. And now she is being punished by being deprived. All this is built into the standard weight-loss diet. The great appeal of the crash/fad diets is that they shorten the period of punishment. Unfortunately, these diets are both potentially dangerous and—usually—ineffective in that the dieter soon gains back the pounds that were shed.

Could I build into a diet enough meaningful rewards to erase the feelings of guilt, deprivation and resentment and replace them with pleasure? Obviously I could not go on daily shopping sprees. What rewards could I offer myself that would turn the process of losing 20 pounds into a pleasure?

A diet, of course, is its own reward in the sense that if one sticks to it, one loses weight. And every weight loss is not only a very meaningful reward in itself, but it also reinforces one's determination to continue.

But it seemed that this reward was not enough. After all, the reward of losing had always been a part of dieting, but I had yet to find anyone who felt that it was enough to turn a diet into a delight. Had I set myself an impossible task? After all, people have been dieting for years, if there was a way to make a diet a pleasure they would have discovered it by now. But perhaps not.

I started a list. What rewards could I give myself that would make me forget that I was being deprived of the amount of food I was accustomed to? What rewards can a diet offer?

1. *A new, trimmer figure.* (Yes, but that was a long-term reward. If I did not have a lot of encouragement

along the way, I might never get there. And besides, as I said, this reward has always been implicit in any diet.)

2. *What about money?* Many of the big international business firms with whom I am associated as a psychological consultant give incentive awards, usually substantial amounts of cash or stock bonuses, to executives who have shown creative initiative. Could I transfer this practice to dieting? (Not bad, but I was used to earning money for positive achievements—for writing, for lecturing, for advising—not for negative achievements like not eating. And I didn't *need* money. It is true that no one ever thinks he or she has enough money—or if there is such a nonmaterialistic soul, I have yet to make his acquaintance, but the fact of giving myself five dollars for every pound I lost, for instance, would be no incentive. Any time I wanted five dollars, I could write out a check. Besides that, this was not a reward that was universally applicable. Many women have to live on such strict budgets that they are lucky if they can squeeze out fifty cents from their food money. And fifty cents is not much of a reward. In addition, the money rewards those executives received came from an outside source, their employer, whatever rewards I was going to build into a diet would have to be supplied by the dieter. That was an important difference.)

3. *Having something nice happen when you lose a pound.* (Yes, this was the real problem. What are the really great universal pleasures of life? I started laughing. One could hardly promise oneself an orgasm per pound lost! Or could one? No. That would mean linking one's sex life to one's diet. Not fair. Because in order for an orgasm to be a reward, this meant no orgasms unless you lose that pound. And if you didn't lose the pound? The dieter punishes not only herself but her sex partner. No, not a good idea. What was the next best thing? It took me

a long time to come up with an answer to that one. Possibly because the answer was so obvious. There is no next best thing to an orgasm.)

I started chewing on my pencil (something no woman in her forties should ever do. Our front incisors get worn down enough without our playing beaver and chewing on wood) . There must be some rewards. The idea of a reward for a pound was good, but I had to lose 20 of them. I had the answer.

4. *A reward for every 3 pounds that are lost.* Now that made sense.

There is a concept in psychology called Goal Gradient, which refers to the pulling power of a goal. In this case, the goal would be that third pound. When you are very close to a goal, research has shown that you pick up speed, you make fewer mistakes, you have an extra spurt of energy.

There have been all sorts of studies that have proven this. A runner who follows a pacer runs much faster than he can when running alone with a stopwatch timing him. A jumper cannot jump as high when he jumps in the air as when he jumps over a bar. The same thing is true of physical labor. In one well-known experiment, researchers used two wheat fields that were exactly the same size. In one field, the researchers placed little red flags at equal intervals; in the other, there were none. Then two teams of farmhands cut the wheat. The men working the field with the red flags (visible goals to work toward) cut the wheat faster and were less tired when they were finished than the men in the other field.

The same Goal Gradient concept applies to mental work as well. When I was teaching at Hunter College, I had two classes that were just about equal in intelligence and ability. I gave them both the same test. With the first group, I simply said, "There is going to be a half-hour test this morning," and handed out the test papers with no further comment. With the second group, I said, "There is going to be a test this morning. I hope you will all do well. I gave it to my earlier class and all of them did surprisingly well. The average mark was ninety-two." This, of course, was not true. I had not even marked the test papers at that time. But the second group, with this high, fictitious average as a goal, did appreciably better than the first class, which had been handed the papers without comment.

Yes, I was on the right track. The Goal Gradient concept would obviously work in dieting.

5. *Not only should one get a reward for every 3 pounds lost, but there should be a bigger reward for every 5 pounds.* (That was it! That would supply two built-in goals for the dieter: the 3-pound goal and the 5-pound goal. There would always be something pulling me along. After I had lost 2½ pounds, it would be no problem for me to stick to the diet long enough to lose that other half pound and get my reward. And every time I had achieved my 3-pound reward, well—I only had 2 more pounds to go to reach that 5-pound goal and the big 5-pound reward. That was it. And knowing myself, I might even manage to go one pound beyond my goal of 20 pounds—in order to get my seventh 3-pound reward.)

But what were the rewards? I had ruled out money. I thought back to the fun I had had on my shopping spree. We all love presents—even if we buy them for ourselves. I belong to a "stocking club" run by a large department store. Every three months they send me three pairs of stockings—and a surprise. And it's the surprise that keeps me a member of the club. It is a convenience, but it is really no problem to run out and buy three pairs of stockings. It's the present that counts. Once it was a tiny handled mirror of imitation tortoise shell, just right for applying eye makeup or checking one's lipstick. Another time it was one of those gadgets that help you pull up a back zipper. The present was always something small, but I really looked forward to it.

What would I look forward to as a 3-pound reward? When I started thinking about it, there were all kinds of small things that I was in the habit of denying myself because I thought they were extravagances. For instance, just a few days ago, I had seen some appealing quilted potholders, but they were three dollars each and I thought that was just too much to spend on a potholder. But now, if I could think of a potholder as a reward, I suspected that the pleasure of seeking out that little shop again and choosing a potholder for kitchen "best," would indeed be a reward.

And what about that silver eyeshadow I had wanted to try, but did not buy because it was "silly." If I felt that I could go ahead and spend money on such a frivolous item, that would be a reward. As I started thinking, there were dozens of little rewards I could conjure up for myself. A new houseplant. I had several coleus (or is it colei), and every time I saw one with a different coloration, I longed for it. A memo pad. I had seen one the other day with DON'T FORGET printed at the top in big red letters. I didn't need a memo pad, but I had thought at the time that it would be kind of fun to have a DON'T FORGET reminder to myself about calling the cleaner, making my airline reservations, getting our dog Joey to the vet for shots—all those things that I was forever jotting down on scraps of paper—and losing.

So that was it. Every time I lost 3 pounds, I could indulge myself in some such minor extravagance. It was not the same as giving myself three or five dollars. Not a bit. That was just money. This way I was giving myself permission to go out, be a little bit extravagant, and do something nice for myself.

But what about the big rewards? The 5-pounders? A 5-pound loss was really worth celebrating. It would take me more than a month if I kept to my lose-one-pound-a-week plan. It was going to be a big event once I got there.

I could not think. I was completely at sea about what kind of reward I should set up for my 5-pound losses. Then I suddenly realized that while a 5-pound loss does not usually affect one's dress size (oh, it may make it fit better or even make it slightly loose), a 10-pound loss will definitely allow the dieter to wear a smaller dress size. That was it! And I could be practical at the same time I was rewarding myself. After all, the whole goal here was to look better. I was not going to be able to run around looking as if I were wearing last year's potato sack.

There were so many clothes and styles that I had passed up because my figure was not good enough. When other women went out at night in well-fitting, black velvet pantsuits or other figure-revealing outfits, I played it safe—and dowdy. No more!

If I lost 5 pounds, I could probably squeeze into a size smaller, although it would not look right on me yet. But I would buy it. Then I would have a really big incentive to lose the next 5 pounds so that I could display my new whatever-it-was on my new slimmer self.

I could hardly wait. My diet was going to be a treat. I almost looked forward to giving up the butter on my vegetables as a concrete step toward being able to run out and get that quilted potholder. Or would I buy the memo pad first? Decisions, decisions. Such delightful decisions!

CHAPTER SIX

The Utterly Delightful Diet

I had settled on my treats. And I knew that I would have to employ a host of tricks to keep myself on a diet and earn those treats. But first I had to work out the diet.

If 1900 calories represented a maintenance diet for me at my present weight, then I had to cut down to 1400 calories a day in order to lose my pound a week. That 500-calorie deficit each day for seven days added up to a 3500-calorie deficit—one pound.

I knew what foods I needed for good health and that a diet, whether it was a weight-loss or a maintenance regime, had to be varied so one could be sure to get all the essential nutrients. But to be on the safe side, I decided to consult Dr. Jean Mayer of Harvard University, one of the country's top nutrition experts.

"What is the wisest diet for women of forty and over?" I asked. "Is there anything special that a woman should eat in order to live longer and keep her looks?"

"You can't give a diet for everyone," Dr. Mayer replied. "Every woman has different needs, a different metabolism, different life-style, different body build, different everything. The only rule I can give that applies to every woman is this: For a long life, you need enough calories, but not too much."

He went on to say, "It is important that a woman's everyday diet be varied to make sure she gets all essential nutrients. It must contain whole-grain cereals or bread, some fruit and vegetables, some protein. It is important to cut down on saturated fats, sugar and salt."

This was solid, conservative advice, but I was a bit disappointed. "There's not much new in what you say, doctor," I told him.

Dr. Mayer retorted rather sharply, "There's not too much new about eating for good health and a long life. But it must be news to most people, because most people eat so poorly."

He was right, of course.

But the important message—what Dr. Mayer was really telling me—was that the individual woman may be her own best dietitian. Knowing her own tastes, problems, lifestyle, activity level, budget (and that is important), weight goal and weaknesses, she can put together a diet that is tailored exactly to her needs.

I already knew my chief weakness. It was going to be difficult to cut down on sweets. While I was intellectually convinced that fruit was a better way of satisfying my cravings for sweets than chocolate cake with a rich icing or a creamy caramel pudding, I just cannot kid myself into thinking that a slice of melon is really dessert. And while I love fresh ripe peaches in season, to my way of thinking they should be accompanied by vanilla ice cream and raspberry sauce. The same goes for strawberries. After all, strawberries and cream have been linked for centuries. I suspect the reason for that is that people worked harder and expended more calories in the daily tasks of living in earlier days. Modern women need very few calories to supply the energy to vacuum the rug and stack the dishwasher.

Unfortunately, my appetite was stuck back in the old days even though my life-style was absolutely 1970's. It was going to be difficult to satisfy that appetite on 1400 calories a day.

As it turned out, it was easier than I had expected to tame my appetite. It was also easier than I had expected to work out a week's diet menus.

Four years at Cornell as a home economics major had taught me a lot about nutrition—so much in fact that there was no reason for my having put on those 20 extra pounds. (No reason except human frailty, and I seem to have my full share of that.) People are often surprised when I tell them I majored in home economics, but there was a very good reason for it. At that time Cornell offered free tuition to women who majored in home economics. Since I was sure I would be running a household one day, I was interested in learning how to do it in the most efficient and effective manner, and since I was also determined to study psychology, it seemed only logical to enroll in home ec— and carry a second major. So I did, although it took some doing. The college authorities were appalled when they learned of my intentions, but I convinced them I could cope—and I did to the tune of almost all A's.

With this background I felt confident that I could plan a well-balanced diet that would include dinner menus that would meet the needs of my husband, who had absolutely no need to diet, and at the same time meet my weight-loss requirements. Since I did not want to deprive myself of my favorite foods, it was a matter of cutting down on the portions I would serve myself.

Using my calorie reference book, it was easy to figure out just how many ounces of this and that I could have— and stay within my caloric limitations. The only real rule I imposed on myself was that I must get all the essential foods into a day's menus before I started trying to squeeze in desserts.

Our weekday breakfast was always the same—freshly squeezed orange juice, coffee with cream and sugar, buttered toast with jam. Milt would occasionally have cold cereal and milk. I decided that I would continue as I had started—simply cutting my normal breakfast in half.

I never included lunch on my menu plans. Neither of us were home during the week and on weekends we slept late and turned breakfast into brunch.

Dinner was the big problem. I had always prepared a good dinner for Milt. Now I would have to prepare a good dinner that would also be a good diet dinner without cutting down on his calories. After all, he did not have an ounce of fat on him. He needed a good solid dinner at night. Because I'm so busy, our dinners usually ran along the lines of lamb chops, broiled fish, liver one night a week, and quite often a broiled capon, which I could cook on my electric spit, basting it occasionally with vermouth and melted butter. There was no reason to change this routine. It was the fried potatoes, the buttery noodles, the rolls and the generous amount of butter I used on vegetables that would have to be adjusted. And I would have to plan desserts that Milt liked and that I could at least have a few spoonfuls of. Fortunately, he liked fruit for dessert better than I did, but I still could not serve fruit every night.

I got out some cookbooks and my box of recipes. I am always clipping recipes that appeal to me, but somehow I never get them filed away on index cards or pasted in my scrapbook. Every once in a while though I go through the carton I store them in and I usually come up with some great new ideas. This time I went fishing for diet recipes.

There were plenty of them—and they all read as if they would be delicious. But as I studied them, it became obvious that there were only a few tricks to most diet recipes. They substituted skim milk for whole milk. They substituted polyunsaturated oil or margarine for butter. They called for artificial sweeteners, which I absolutely would not consider using.

When I analyzed them, the main requirements for a diet recipe were that it start with low-calorie ingredients—like fish, for instance—and that the cooked dish be served in small portions. I did not need special diet recipes to help me employ those two principles. Nor does any woman who is at home in the kitchen.

I had already made a practice of using polyunsaturated oil in salads, because I was interested in keeping my husband's cholesterol count low. He had never had a high reading, probably because he exercised so much, but I did not believe in taking chances. I also used skim milk in cooking, although I preferred whole milk for drinking. The upshot of my short research into diet recipes was a decision to cook as I had always cooked and to diet, just as I had started, by cutting down my portions. Only now that I had my Diet Trousseau, I could cut down my portions intelligently and not just by guess. With my new food scale, my measuring cup and spoons, and my calorie tables, I could easily control the amount of calories I ate at dinner.

The point of all this is that a woman can diet on spaghetti and meatballs or on lettuce and grapefruit, just as long as she makes sure that her diet includes all the basic nutritional building blocks. After that, it is simply a matter of measuring the caloric content of the helpings you allow yourself.

My diet was going to be just what my diet had been in

the past; only the amounts I served myself would be changed. And, yes, I decided it would be a long time before I served chocolate mousse with whipped cream again. After all, I wanted those rewards I had promised myself.

CHAPTER SEVEN

Diet Traps and Tricks

The course of true love, they say, never runs smooth. Neither does that of a diet. A diet—for me at any rate—is full of big and little booby traps, all sorts of obstacles. And I needed a whole bag of tricks to cope with them—especially since I insisted that my diet be as delightful as possible.

Because of the world food shortages and the number of people who are starving or living at bare subsistence levels, I feel ashamed of myself for making a big deal out of living on a carefully thought-out diet that supplies all the food values I need for good skin, strong bones, plentiful energy and all that makes up sturdy good health, while other women are begging for food for their swollen-bellied, listless babies. And yet, I have to confess that this horror wears off and I have to keep reminding myself of it. It seems to be just too much for one person to cope with for long. I suggest that all of us women who have led such comfortable lives that we must now lose weight would do well not to feel too sorry for ourselves. Other women are starving to death.

I hesitate to introduce this grim note into a book that is designed as a guide to making the most of one's second-chance years, but this is the world we live in. It is important to keep an honest perspective on our lives. I hope that all of us in our second-chance years will spend some of our accumulated wisdom, our increased freedom and our energy working to help these other women, working to end famines and starvation.

And as a small rationale for spending so much time and energy on ourselves now, the kind of woman who can help deal with these problems is the woman who is at her physical, mental and emotional peak. I hope this book will help women reach these peaks, and any tricks that are used should be considered constructive steps toward an admirable goal.

The first trick was purely psychological—eating from smaller dishes. My initial half-portion dinner made me feel like poor Oliver Twist. I wanted MORE. There was so much plate—and so little food. But there is no law that says one must eat dinner from a dinner plate. Nor drink one's morning coffee from a big breakfast cup. So, I rummaged through my china closet and chose a dessert plate to serve as my dinner plate. It made my pitiful two ounces of this and three ounces of that appear like generous helpings. And while it may seem silly to pour breakfast coffee into a demitasse, the doll-sized cup let me enjoy my coffee laced with the same proportion of cream and sugar I used to. The small size also resulted in reducing my morning gulps of coffee to ladylike sips. An important factor in a diet, as I shall explain later in this chapter.

As tricks go, this was relatively straightforward, but it was good enough to fool me. It worked. As long as my plate was full, I did not feel deprived.

One of the most effective tricks is to keep the thermostat turned down in the cold weather. A temperature of 62° or 64° will not only cut down on your fuel bill, it will force your body to burn up calories faster to keep warm—and help you live longer. That's right. Studies have shown that a cool environment is conducive to longer life. If you feel chilly, wear a sweater and exercise. There's a very good, fast warm-up exercise that takes only a minute (see page 88).

I lost 2 pounds the first week, one more than my goal. Most women find that even though they may only cut down by the magic 3500 calories (a pound's worth), 2 and sometimes 3 pounds melt away the first week. This is because cutting down on food seems to trigger a change in body chemistry that affects water retention during the first few days. It is as if your body is trying to encourage you.

And when I earned that first 3-pound reward after only two weeks, it was another big boost. I was really triumphant. I treated myself to that silver eyeshadow that I had wanted to buy before but had not because it was "too silly" (more about this silver dust in Chapter Eleven, Artist at Work).

I reached my 5-pound goal in exactly one month—and the same day got a wonderful, ego-boosting compliment that was a reward in itself. The stylist on our show said, "You're losing weight, aren't you? If you keep it up, I'm going to have to get a smaller size for you. You know," she went on, "you are looking absolutely glowing these days. You must have a lover."

I laughed. "That's my secret."

I was not going to tell the world I was dieting. If people thought that love was making me thin, well, that was fine with me. And in a way, it was true. I did have a demanding lover. There was something going on between Milt and myself that was exciting—and unexpected after twenty-five years of marriage (see Chapter Fifteen). Incidentally, an active sex life is a great diet aid. Lovemaking burns up 150 calories (200 if it's superspecial).

That 5-pound loss posed an absolutely delightful problem. What to buy? I wanted to build in a strong Goal Gradient incentive to help me lose the next 5 pounds. I decided to get something absolutely smashing for evening wear, something that would make people look twice.

After a long afternoon of shopping when I wriggled in and out of so many beautiful costumes that I began to wonder if anyone had ever figured how many calories trying on clothes burned up, I found exactly what I wanted—something I would never have dreamed of buying before. A pair of evening pajamas in a fragile, feather-printed chiffon, transparent in all the right places. They could not have been more becoming—or daring. Every move set off a very feminine, very dramatic flutter of chiffon panels.

"I'll take it," I said, "but I want a size smaller."

The saleswoman opened her mouth, then quickly closed it. I could tell that she was reminding herself, "The customer is always right," as she shook her head and took that one-size-too-small creation off to be wrapped in layers of tissue. When I unwrapped it at home, I felt a little panicky. It had been *very* expensive. Extravagant was the word. Would I ever lose enough to wear it? Right now, I could just squeeze into it, but could not fasten the delicate little snaps and tiny hooks. It was not so much that I looked "poured into" the outfit, but that I was bulging out of it. I had to lose weight, just had to. Those pajamas were an expensive come-on, a kind of diet "carrot"—and I was the donkey yearning after that carrot.

As it turned out, they were worth every pretty penny they cost. I needed all the pulling power a goal could give me plus a few tricks to lose the next 5 pounds. Along about the end of the sixth week, I started cheating. I nibbled my way past the 1400 mark up to 1800 . . . 2000 . . . 2500 calories. When I added them up, I would be desperately ashamed, but I kept on nibbling.

At meals, I would measure out my diet portions—three ounces of this, a quarter of a cup of that—but afterwards in the kitchen when I was cleaning up, I would have another slice of meat, a cookie, anything that was left over. It got so that my after-dinner snacking added up to more calories than my dinner. Between meals I had cravings for a chocolate bar, a bag of potato chips, a piece of coconut layer cake—and I indulged them, feeling guilty as hell with every mouthful but not letting that stop me.

When I went over to Milt's office and weighed myself on his medical scale at the end of the seventh week, it told the inflationary truth—the same story my bathroom scales had been telling me. I had gained 2 pounds during the seventh week of the diet instead of losing one. I felt awful. Guilty. Fat. Seven weeks of dieting and only 5 pounds to show for it. If it had not been for that serendipitous loss of 2 pounds in the first week, I would have only lost 4 pounds in seven weeks. Surely a pound a week—a mere 3500 calories less— was not too much to demand of myself. I could not understand. How had I been able to get along so well for about six weeks and then start backsliding?

Was I going to fail? Give up on my diet after all the planning that had gone into it? After all the money I had spent on my Diet Trousseau? I had a big emotional stake in losing those 20 pounds. If I failed it would be like sentencing myself to a dowdy middle age. And I could forget about the butterfly years. I didn't deserve them.

No, I couldn't let myself down. I wouldn't. I was not going to miss my butterfly years. And I really thought of it in those terms. I was convinced that if I let myself settle for being overweight and looking less than my best that it was the equivalent of saying, "I give up. It is all downhill from now on."

The very thought scared me enough to work out another diet trick. This one was a combination diagnostic tool and consciousness-raiser—my Diet Diary, that little blue-and-white notebook that was part of my Diet Trousseau. I had been making entries in it every day, or almost every day, but this had been a "bright idea" that did not seem to be working out the way I had hoped. Once I had worked out some 1400-calorie menus and knew pretty well what was allowed within that limit, I got bored with jotting down my daily intake. As for those forbidden nibbles, I am afraid I played the ostrich game. I just did not write them down on the idea that what I didn't record didn't count. That was a big mistake and was why the diary was not working for me. I was not taking it seriously. I was not using it correctly. I was not telling "Dear Diary" the truth.

A Diet Diary can be the dieter's best friend. It is an even better reflection of the total woman than her mirror, because, used correctly, it can reflect the future. I urge all dieting women to learn from my experience and make use of their Diet Diaries. Set your own diary up any way that works for you. Here is a sample from mine during that period when I was nibbling on forbidden foods and had finally decided to tell the truth—to my friend, the Diet Diary.

WEDNESDAY

Up at 7:00
Weighed 122¼
Drank big glass of water with my vitamin pills

Breakfast at 7:30

4 ounces orange juice	55 calories
1 slice whole wheat toast	75
whipped butter	20
strawberry jam	20
one tablespoon of cream	40
one teaspoon of sugar	18
one strip of bacon	50

Business conference at 10:45

Coffee with cream and sugar	50
pastry (I was absolutely starving)	350

Lunch at 1:15

carton of yogurt	130
apple	80

Afternoon snack around 4:30 when I got home and felt very, very hungry

Tea	00
English muffin with butter	200

Dinner (just the two of us at 8:00. Milt was late and I was starving again)

slice of calf's liver	300
half a cup of broccoli with lemon juice	25
mashed potato with milk and butter	100
big helping of spinach salad with oil and vinegar and bacon bits	100
orange sherbet on a slice of fresh pineapple	225
2 cookies	70

And so to bed around midnight

small glass of milk	80
chocolate graham cracker	50

There it was—more than 2100 calories. Seven hundred above my limit. (My calorie count may not have been completely accurate, but it was accurate enough—and the addition was absolutely correct. I had my toy, the small electronic calculator, which toted up the caloric bad news.) Those midmorning and midafternoon snacks had added up to 600 calories, almost half my daily allotment. And the cookies at dinner, plus the graham cracker at bedtime, had added another 120 calories. A grand total of 720 unnecessary calories. Illegitimate calories was the way I thought of them.

Day after day, the diary showed the same pattern of snacking on sweets. It was easy enough to see where I was having trouble. I also consistently reported that I was "starving."

That necessary element of "utter delight" had vanished from my diet. But the diary pointed to an obvious solution.

On that particular Wednesday, I might have been able to resist the pastry with my midmorning coffee if I had known I would have a satisfying lunch in an hour or so. Yogurt and an apple does not add up to a satisfying lunch. And if I had not been so hungry after my meager lunch, I might have been able to resist that buttery muffin I gobbled down with my tea in the afternoon.

The solution was staring me in the face. Yogurt and an apple were not enough for lunch, not enough to keep me fueled up during a long, busy day. It was time for a change —or two.

The first change was to institute a legitimate midmorning snack. I would have yogurt at eleven—130 healthy calories.

The second change was lunch. It had to be something more solid. I settled on a three-ounce can of tuna fish, a few sprigs of watercress, two pieces of whole wheat melba toast and an apple.* This added up to about 235 calories. I kept a can opener at the studio and bought a package of plastic forks so I could eat the tuna fish out of the can. Not elegant, I admit, but practical. When I told an executive at NBC about my "brown bag lunches," he confessed that he brown-bagged it, too, with a couple of slices of chicken or a hard-boiled egg, a plastic cup of cottage cheese and carrot sticks.

This got me out of that diet slump. I had learned the hard way just how easy it is to put on a pound without even trying. I had also learned not to let myself get so hungry that I stuffed myself with illegitimate high-calorie sweets. I was beginning to learn the lesson—really learn it, I mean—that the dieter must make sure that every mouthful she eats packs a nutritional boost. There is very little room on a diet for those illegitimate empty calories.

The next diet trap was a frustrating plateau. I was sticking to the diet. I doled out calories to myself like the stingiest of Scrooges doling out sixpences, but I just could not seem to lose. Or very little. Instead of a pound a week, I could just barely lose half a pound.

What was happening? I reviewed my Diet Diary. No in-

---

* Another trick seems very obvious, but if you omit it, you may fall into a trap. And that's planning menus—and sticking to them. On a long-term diet, it is very easy to fall into the trap of feeling that you know it all. You know your calorie counts, you know what you should eat and what you should not, so you kind of fly by the seat of your pants. The trouble with that kind of flying and that kind of dieting is that you often don't reach your destination. Our minds play tricks on us. We conveniently forget what we don't want to know. We forget the butter we spread on the bread, the little sample of cheese and crackers that was given away at the supermarket, the handful of nuts we ate at a cocktail party. They all count. So make a menu. It's more efficient and better for the budget if you do your menu planning by the week. And don't, don't, don't eat anything that's not on your menu. That way lies diet disaster.

discretions there. Every nibble had been noted and the total was usually just a few calories over or under the 1400. What was wrong?

Suddenly it dawned on me. I had lost 11 pounds by now. Of course! The more weight you lose, the fewer calories you need to maintain your new weight. And to lose *more* weight, you need even *fewer* calories than before.

This booby trap, even more dangerous than the sixth- or seventh-week slump, lies in wait for every long-term dieter. It is important to know about it. It can be discouraging to diet day after day and lose only ounces instead of pounds. This is when the majority of dieters give up. They think they have reached some magic barrier which is impossible to pass.

True enough, it is a barrier, but there is nothing magic about it. They have reached the point where they need less food. It is a sign of success, which means that they have to readjust their diets to their new weight. These plateaus come at about every 10-pound loss, so this means a diet must be reviewed and adjusted at every 10 pounds.

Cutting down is not as difficult as one might think if the dieter has been on the slow-but-sure, lose-one-pound-a-week diet. During the ten weeks it takes to lose 10 pounds, the body has had time to adjust itself. A new eating pattern has been established—not strongly, it still needs reinforcement—but dieters discover that they no longer crave the amount of food they used to eat. In fact, they find that if they revert to their old eating habits for even one meal, they feel uncomfortable.

I still had 9 pounds to lose. I would cut down by another 100 calories a day and see how that worked out. According to the diet charts, I needed about 1800 calories to maintain my present 117 pounds. Cutting back to a 1300-calorie-a-day diet would give me the 3500-a-week deficit that I needed to keep on losing a pound a week.

(Most diet charts, of course, are only approximate. So much depends on the dieter's age, body build, daily energy output and a host of other things besides the height and weight criteria most charts are based on, that the charts found in diet books and magazines cannot be considered as gospel. The best guide of all is the informed dieter's own common sense and self-knowledge.)

But what more could I give up?

The cream in my coffee, for one thing. A few weeks ago I would have fought to keep that cream, but now my taste and needs seemed to be changing. I no longer liked cream and butter as much as I used to. It was easy to use milk in my coffee instead of cream. It also turned out to be no hardship to drink skim milk at bedtime instead of whole milk. My body was beginning to tell me what was good for it—and what was good for it was less fat: less cream, less butter, less whole milk.

I still liked the flavor of butter, but I discovered a way to enjoy the taste and skip many calories. I switched to whipped butter and made it even less caloric by turning the little tub of whipped butter into the bowl of my electric mixer and whipping ice water into it—as much as it would hold. This gave more volume and resulted in fewer calories per spoonful. A tablespoon of regular butter is about 100 calories. A tablespoon of whipped butter is about 70 calories. With the extra air and water I whipped into mine, the calorie count was even lower.

I played other little tricks on myself. I found a gadget that held a normal slice of bread so that one could slice it in half. Now I could make a sandwich using only one slice of bread.

Milt used to ask, "Why don't you simply fold the slice of bread over and make half a sandwich instead of going to all that trouble to split the slice and make it look like a complete sandwich?"

It just would not have been the same thing. I would have thought I was only getting half a sandwich if I folded the bread over—and that would have made me feel deprived. In the same way, I feel fuller after eating three sliver-thin slices of chicken than if I eat one slice of chicken that weighs as much as the three slivers put together.

I suspect this has something to do with the child who still exists within each of us—and that child's confusion about the concepts of volume and space.

In one experiment illustrating this confusion, researchers showed children a drinking glass full of water. Then they placed a tall, slim glass vase containing the same amount of water beside the drinking glass.

Each child was asked, "Which holds more water? The glass? Or the vase?"

Each child invariably pointed to the vase. It was taller than the drinking glass so they reasoned it "must" hold more water.

In another experiment, a teacher placed two sticks of modeling clay on the table.

"Which stick is bigger?" she asked.

"They are both the same size," the students answered.

"That's right," said the teacher. "They are both the same size. Now watch me."

She took one stick of the clay and shaped it into a ball. Then she rolled the other stick into a long, round "snake."

"Now which is bigger?" she asked.

Without exception the children agreed that the "snake"

was bigger than the ball—despite the fact they had observed the teacher form both from equal-sized sticks of clay.

It is not until a child is 9 or even 10 years old that he is able to understand that the shape of a given substance may be altered, but the volume stays the same. And this may be the reason why it is easy to convince myself that three sliver-sized slices of chicken seem like a lot more to eat than the same amount of chicken in one piece. Or why I feel I have more when I split a slice of bread into two skinny slices than when I fold that same slice over to make a sandwich.

A variation of the same principle applies to my morning demitasse. When I sip it, I feel I have had as much coffee as I used to have in my big breakfast cup when I used to gulp down the coffee to wake myself up. The number of sips is roughly equivalent to the old number of gulps—and that seems to satisfy me—almost.

The skinny slices of bread definitely satisfied me. On Sundays, I used to cut a hole in the middle of one with a cookie cutter, place the bread in my Teflon frying pan, then crack an egg and place it in the hole. In a minute, I had a piece of toasted bread with a fried egg in the center. It looked and tasted like a very hearty Sunday breakfast, but was really very calorie thrifty. Even when served with my Sunday slice of bacon.

I learned to separate bacon strips and pour boiling water over the ones I was going to fry to melt away the fat. I bought a bacon griddle that was made on a slant so that as the bacon cooked the fat ran off down into a corner of the pan. This way the bacon did not fry in its own fat and cooked up quite dry. I would blot it on a paper towel before serving to get the last bit of fat off.

How many calories did I save with these little tricks? I don't know, but I know I saved some. And saved them painlessly.

Other calorie-cutting tricks I developed were to just use a few drops of oil in my oil and vinegar salad dressing (the proportion is something like 12 to 1 in favor of vinegar), to order less expensive cuts of beef because they contained less fat, to cut the amount of sugar I used in coffee in half again. None of these tricks saved more than a few calories, but 10 calories here and 15 there added up to substantial savings over the course of a week. Almost equally important, these tricks kept me from feeling deprived by letting me follow my established eating patterns until—as in the case of butter and whole milk—my body let me know that it wanted a change.

The greatest problem I faced was my appetite. As I have said, all my life I have had a good appetite. Now it seemed that more and more often I was getting up from the table feeling almost as hungry as when I sat down. This was an unwelcome development. Here I had worked hard to devise a diet that would be enjoyable. For the most part, I had succeeded. I seldom felt deprived and each weight-loss goal that I reached was truly a delightful milestone.

Now, when I was more than halfway to my 20-pound goal, I was beset by gnawing hunger. Not delightful at all. It was beginning to take real willpower and self-discipline to stay on my 1300-calorie regime. This was not what I called delightful. Something had to be done.

My inclination is always to consult the experts and that is what I did. I read up on the latest findings in medical and nutritional journals and then talked to the researchers who had been responsible for these findings. Out of all this came a simple discovery—but so effective that there is no reason for anyone who uses this trick to get up from the

DIET TRAPS AND TRICKS   61

table feeling hungry. And it does not involve eating more.

The trick, or the discovery, and it could not be simpler, is—Slow Down!

I discovered that by eating more slowly, I felt full sooner and never finished a meal feeling that I'd like to start all over again. There is a reason for this—one that all dieters should be aware of. It takes from 20 to 30 minutes for your body to signal your brain that you are no longer hungry. Therefore it is important to eat slowly enough so that your brain gets the message that you are full and stops sending "hungry" signals. It is perfectly easy to trick your brain into cutting down on these "I'm starving" signals. I worked out a program of eating that did just this.

Before dinner, just before Milt was due to walk in the door, I made myself a cup of broth with a bouillon cube and boiling water. Total calories: 8. I would sip this slowly (I had to, it was so hot). Then I would progress to a bit of solid food. Not *with* the bouillon, but *after* it. The time lag is important. I was giving my body time to flash the signal to my brain that it was getting food. I would prepare celery and carrot sticks, wash a few sprigs of watercress and parsley and set out a tray for myself. It was very relaxing to munch on my low-low-calorie snacks and sip a glass of club soda with a twist of lemon while Milt was having his before-dinner drink. Sometimes I made small "rabbit sandwiches," tucking a sprig or two of parsley into the hollow of the celery and topping it with a carrot sliver. A sprinkle of chopped chives added flavor. Occasionally I would indulge myself and add a spoonful of skimmed-milk cottage cheese. The liquid from the bouillon and the club soda helped make me feel full (I'd always have to make a trip to the bathroom before sitting down to dinner), and the rabbit food convinced me that I was getting something solid to eat. This slow approach to the dinner table helped.

By the time we sat down to eat, I was no longer starving hungry. I could eat more slowly. I also found that it helped to eat some starchy food first. If I began with my half a baked potato or my half cup of rice and ate a few mouthfuls before touching the meat or vegetables, that seemed to help.

It also helps to plan menus around "slow-to-eat" foods. One of my favorites starts with artichokes, which are only 80 to 90 calories, and take forever to eat. If you dip each leaf in lemon juice, there are no additional calories. If, like me, you want something more, use this calorie-saving sauce. I mix two tablespoons of plain yogurt, a teaspoon of mayonnaise and the juice of half a lemon or some white wine vinegar—enough to make it very runny. This adds less than 50 calories.

I usually follow this with veal scaloppine. I pound the veal very thin and sauté it in about a quarter of a teaspoon of butter in my Teflon pan. Before serving, I squeeze a few drops of lemon juice over it. I add pepper, sometimes a sprinkling of chives. I do not salt it. (Milt will ask for salt at the table, he always does. This way, by not salting it earlier, I think I keep his salt consumption down as well as mine.) My two- to three-ounce portion is somewhere around 175 calories. I serve a green salad as a separate third course, another trick that slows down a meal.

My favorite dessert with this is strawberries with their stems left on. I dip them one by one into a little crystal bowl of fresh orange juice and I allow myself one plain cookie.

Whether for myself or for guests, this is a delicious and very satisfactory dinner because you can eat it slowly without seeming to stall. (You'd be surprised how the minutes go by as one nibbles on an artichoke leaf or a strawberry.) And best of all, it counts out under 450 calories.

Another trick to slow one down is the counting trick. Whenever I found myself eating faster than I should, I made a point of putting down my fork and counting (silently) to 30. It is perfectly possible to do this and still pay attention to what your dinner partner is saying. This 30 count was an effective brake.

When I caught myself eating too fast when I was alone, I used another trick. I propped a mirror up in front of me at the table. It is impossible to eat fast once you catch sight of the way you look shoveling the food in.

Another trick I learned, especially on those evenings when Milt played squash and I ate by myself, was to *always* set a place for myself and sit down at the table to eat. There is something about standing at the kitchen counter with the refrigerator door open and having a bite of this and a swallow of that, instead of serving yourself a proper meal, that is absolutely destructive to a diet. The same rule applies to eating ice cream out of the carton, for instance. If you must have ice cream, scoop it out into a dish, then sit down and eat it. It will be more satisfying, and you will eat less.

I also discovered another reason for those hunger pangs. The dieter who gets plenty of sleep does not feel as hungry as the dieter who does not get enough. Researchers have learned that dieters dream about food more than non-dieters. That is easy enough to understand, but what was not understood until recently is that those food dreams are very important to the dieter.

Most dreams occur during the period of light sleep that scientists call REM (Rapid Eye Movement) sleep. In one study, researchers kept waking dieters every time they entered the period of REM sleep. This effectively interrupted the dieters' dreams. These dieters experienced almost uncontrollable hunger feelings the day after their sleep was interrupted and most of them ate much more than they should have.

It is important to have plenty of good sleep, otherwise it may be impossible to suppress the hunger impetus that comes from within the brain. If you are constantly hungry, you may not be enjoying your full quota of food dreams. In this case, it would be wise to make sure you go to bed early enough to get a full night's sleep. If you have difficulty in falling asleep, get into the habit of drinking a glass of milk before going to bed. It is extremely sleep conducive. Exercise also acts as a physical and emotional tranquilizer and makes sleep come more easily, especially such stretching exercises as Yoga. And making love at bedtime almost always works (if you're alone or if nightly lovemaking is too much for your husband, there is nothing wrong with masturbating to a relaxing bedtime orgasm—the very best kind of "sleeping pill").

The next diet trap—and the hardest one of all to deal with—was boredom. I was bored with my nourishing, low-calorie meals. I yearned for a bag of peanuts, a chocolate sundae with torrents of chocolate sauce and gobs of whipped cream. I dreamed of black bean soup and hot buttery rolls and mountains of chili with saltines on the side. The food commercials on television drove me crazy. I'd find myself salivating when they showed a plate of french fries. My trips to the supermarket were cruel temptations.

I tried reminding myself how well I had done. I would take out my Diet Diary and look over the long weeks of dieting with the red-letter days when I achieved my 3-pound and 5-pound rewards. I would think of the compliments I was getting on how well I looked. I would think of the new interest in my husband's eyes. And then I would think of a peanut-butter sandwich—maybe with Marshmallow Fluff.

I tried discipline. Whenever my thoughts wandered to food, I would get busy. I cleaned out all my closets and packed up the clothes that were too big for me to give to the Salvation Army and Goodwill Industries. That helped, but there was a limit to my closets—and to the clothes I could give away.

I would call up a friend or my sister or my parents and chat for ten minutes. That often got my mind off food.

One trick to keep the bored dieter on the straight and narrow is to have her husband (or a close friend—he'd better be close) take some nude pictures of her before she starts the diet. From the front and the side. Just one look at the pictures should be enough to banish boredom and make the diet more appealing. Every time the dieter feels her resolve weakening, she should take out the pictures and study them carefully.

It may also help to repeat the photography sessions at each 5-pound loss. The graphic evidence of improvement will also act as an incentive.

My best weapon turned out to be the movies. On the nights that Milt played squash, I often went to the movies right after dinner. Sometimes I would take my dessert with me—a sliced apple or ten cherries or ten strawberries in a plastic bag. I would eat them slice by slice, cherry by cherry, trying to make them last as long as possible. This worked very well. I'd forget all about food if the movie was really good and be surprised to discover that I still had a few strawberries left.

But no matter what I tried, I still yearned for a creamy sauce on my chicken breast. I wanted my tuna fish buried in mayonnaise. I wanted pancakes drowning in syrup.

There was no point in being miserable; it was time for another change. I would settle for losing half a pound a week from now on. At this point I had only 6 pounds to go. Besides that, I had noticed that I was getting just a little flabby here and there. My upper arms were no longer chubby, but while slimming down they had developed just the slightest sag. Same with my thighs. And my stomach— well, it was not as flat as I had hoped it would be. A slower rate of weight loss might give my skin and muscles the chance they needed to adjust to the new smaller me.

I worked out a new Goal Gradient approach. Oh, I wasn't going to give up my 3- and 5-pound rewards; I was going to add another treat—something I seemed to want more than anything else in the world at this point. Food.

Using the Goal Gradient Principle, it seemed to me that it would be much easier to diet if I had a surefire, immediate goal or reward. I decided to try a Two-Days-On-and-One-Day-Off Diet; I would stay with 1300 calories a day for two days, then on the third I would allow myself 1800. The extra 500 calories could be spent in any madcap manner I wanted.

It is important to understand that there is an element of danger in setting up food as a reward on a diet. After all, too many of us are on diets because we had gotten in the habit of using food to comfort ourselves or reward ourselves or generally make up to ourselves for something that was not quite right in our lives. Many women can trace their overweight directly to being rewarded for good behavior with an extra piece of cake or money for an ice-cream cone when they were children. On the other hand, we women of 40 and over know ourselves pretty well. And there is no particular advantage in *punishing* ourselves by withholding food, either. The effective diet, the successful diet, is one that will leave a woman thinner and more capable of controlling her feelings about food than she was when she started. So while one should not go overboard about using food as a reward for successful dieting, neither should one bend over backward and deprive oneself of food as a punishment.

Those extra 500 calories every third day simply place the dieter on a *maintenance* diet instead of a weight-loss diet. She will not gain weight; she will simply lose at a slightly slower rate. This turning every third day into a maintenance day can be an excellent idea toward the end of a long diet. It eases the dieter into what will be her normal eating pattern for most of the rest of her life.

The wise dieter will try hard to avoid the empty-calorie trap when she treats herself to those 500 bonus calories every third day. Since I have such a sweet tooth, I decided to restrict myself to homemade desserts to satisfy that sweet tooth and keep empty calories to a minimum. I bought a home ice-cream freezer, one of those small cylinders that buzz away in your freezing compartment and turn out a quart of pure ice cream. My favorite flavors were fresh strawberry, peach, orange sherbet and a marvelous concoction I found in a health-food cookbook with honey, sesame seeds and sunflower seeds.

I also started making cookies for my third-day treats. I had always baked cookies for Lisa and her friends, but now I was doing it for myself. But no more brownies or Tollhouse cookies. Now I was baking oatmeal cookies with raisins and nuts and wheat germ.

Since I had given myself "permission" to eat something sweet, I was content with these healthy sweets. (Not that I have given up chocolate and whipped cream. I still indulge—but very, very rarely. Only as a special treat. And that's the way it should be.)

The third-day treat is an extremely effective way of

fighting boredom as well as reeducating the dieter for re-
entry into normal eating. If you think of it, the fact that
the dieter can accept a normal maintenance diet as a treat
is a wonderful achievement.

Now that the ounces were melting away at a slower rate,
I got impatient. And I was unhappy with my body. I was
close to my 20-pound goal, but my body wasn't what it had
been when I was 20—or when I was 30.

There was a certain flabbiness and as I twisted around in
the mirror, I could swear that my buttocks were drooping!
It was all very depressing. I had expected some magic
transformation, even though I knew better. By losing
weight I had thought I would look the way I did when I
weighed 108 pounds and was 20 years old. But I didn't. It
didn't make sense. I knew better. But I was depressed.

Then I hit on a solution—no, it didn't make me look 20
again, but it did make me look younger and at the same
time allowed me to eat a hearty 1700 calories a day and
still lose one pound a week. I'll tell you about this solution
in Chapter Nine. (If you can't wait, there's no harm in
skipping the following chapter and coming back to it
later.)

CHAPTER EIGHT

The Ten Questions
People Ask Me About Dieting

In the course of a year, I give about 220 lectures to groups all over the United States. My audiences range from podiatrists to prep schools, from floor-covering distributors to Junior Leagues. And after each lecture there is a question period. No matter what my subject has been, many of the questions are about dieting. This is probably the most diet-conscious nation in the world—and well it should be. Statistics show that at least 75 million (and possibly more than 100 million) Americans weigh more than they should for their own good. Here are the ten questions I'm asked most frequently about dieting:

1. *What about drinking and dieting?*

It is like drinking and driving. Don't mix them. Drinking while on a diet is bad calorically, bad for your health and terrible for your looks.

Ever since some of those crash-fad diets based on exaggeratedly high-protein, low-carbohydrate combinations that permitted the dieter to drink, people have tended to believe that by some magic chemistry alcohol calories don't count for dieters. They do. They count a lot. One ounce of 86-proof Scotch, bourbon, rye, gin, vodka, tequila, rum or brandy represents 50 calories, and most drinks contain one and a half ounces of liquor. Wine calories count, too. A three-ounce glass of a dry red or dry white wine or a dry champagne averages about 75 calories. Sweeter wines have a higher calorie count. And three ounces of wine are not very much. Take your Diet Trousseau measuring cup and pour three ounces of water into a wine glass. It looks pretty stingy.

It's not only the empty calories that are dangerous. Alcohol can endanger your health. In one representative study, a group of normal, healthy adults on a low-calorie diet were given carefully controlled amounts of alcohol. Most of them developed significant symptoms of hypogly-cemia (a metabolic disturbance in which blood glucose levels become dangerously low). The individuals who were affected suddenly felt weak, nervous and headachy. Most of them felt extremely shaky. Some vomited. Some sweated profusely. When tested, their motor skills were "weak and erratic."

Most physicians who put patients on diets caution them against drinking. One highly respected diet specialist tells women who insist that they will not give up liquor (and I am not talking about alcoholics, simply women who like their cocktails before dinner or wine with meals) that they can have *one* drink every *three* days. And by one drink, this doctor means one ounce of hard liquor or three ounces of wine. No more. And he does not have my "third-day treat" in mind; he is simply convinced that this is the maximum amount of alcohol a woman over 38 to 40 should drink while dieting.

And then there is the matter of how you look when you drink. Psychologists have found that men drink to feel powerful and women drink to feel feminine and sexy (an-other form of power), but that in both cases, this is a self-defeating exercise. The more a man drinks the less control he has; and the more a woman drinks, the less attractive she is. Check this out at cocktail parties for yourself. The women over 38 to 40 who have more than one drink usually leave looking much less attractive than when they entered. One's tolerance for liquor also diminishes and drinking tends to trigger unpleasant behavior—talking too loudly or too much, aggressiveness, flirtatiousness, all sorts of ridiculous behavior. The woman who is serious about making the most of her second-chance years certainly does not want to waste even a minute of them making a fool of herself.

When I go to cocktail parties, I sip a glass of club soda with a twist of lemon in it. It gives me something to do with my hands, others think I'm having some gin or vodka mixture—and it never goes to my head.

Does this mean that women should give up drinking? Yes, absolutely, if they are dieting. If they are not, my feeling—although I do not drink myself—is that alcohol in moderation can be a blessing. Wine is relaxing. Doctors often prescribe whiskey for patients with circulatory problems. But the key is moderation.

2. *What's the best time to start a diet?*

Twenty-four hours from now. There is a psychological advantage in taking twenty-four hours to prepare for a diet. If you take time to decide just how much weight you should lose, how long it should take you to lose it, to accumulate your Diet Trousseau, to set goals for yourself in order to take advantage of the Goal Gradient Principle (see page 37), and to work out menus, this will pay real diet dividends. The thought, time and money you have invested in your diet project will pay dividends. It's just like any other investment, you will work to make it profitable.

But don't wait more than twenty-four hours. And, above all, don't let the "if onlies" stop you from starting. You know what they are:

"If only I weren't so busy right now."

"If only I weren't so worried about money right now."

"If only I didn't have to cook for the whole family."

"If only I weren't so upset about my son right now."

These "if onlies" will never go away. The thing is to ignore them and start your diet—twenty-four hours from now.

3. *What about eating out when you're on a diet?*

It is really not a problem. I know, because I travel so much I eat out more than I like. Once you have been on your diet for ten days to two weeks, you will be very familiar with the calorie counts of most foods that you eat. And if you have used your food scale conscientiously, you will be able to judge fairly accurately just what three or four ounces of roast beef or steak or lamb chop or chicken look like. What I did when I first started my diet was to weigh my three-ounce portions of meat on my food scale. When I had exactly three ounces of chicken, for instance, I picked it up and put it in the palm of my hand. It really wasn't very much. But that helped me visualize what three ounces of meat looked like (beef and chicken weigh roughly the same), and this helped me at the beginning. No, I didn't pick up my slice of roast beef in the restaurant, but I did hold my hand over it—sort of as if I were giving it a blessing. And I never hesitate to ask for a "doggie bag" for the rest of my meat. I've paid for it and it usually supplies a good diet portion for the following day.

When I fly, I always carry my own yogurt and some fruit. Airline food is simply terrible. I much prefer my Spartan diet snacks.

Jacqueline Kennedy Onassis, who went on a stringent

diet and exercise program when she reached 40, had a favorite diet meal she ordered when she went out in the evening: a baked potato split and heaped high with fresh caviar accompanied by champagne. This extravagant meal is actually calorie thrifty. An enormous baked potato may run up to 150 calories. An ounce of caviar is 75 calories—and two ounces would be an extremely generous helping. Two glasses of champagne would come to about 250 calories.

Not all of us have caviar and champagne tastes—or pocketbooks. One of my favorite eating-out meals is chef's salad. I always ask that the dressing be served on the side so that I can monitor how much I eat. An omelet is high in protein and low in calories and makes a good lunch along with a plain green salad. Once you become sophisticated about calorie counts, it is not at all hard to eat out on a diet.

4. *Aren't there some people who are predisposed to fat, who are doomed to be "forever fat"?*

Yes. And no. There are very few. There is a handful of people with glandular disturbances, but this is really not a significant segment of the overweight population. And then there are some—and this is also a tiny proportion of the overweight population—who are doomed to work harder than the rest of us to keep their weight within the normal range. These are people who were overfed as infants. As a result, they developed more fat cells than babies who were fed correctly. The problem is that fat cells never go away. Even when these individuals go on diets and lose weight when they are grown-up, the fat cells are still there crying out to be fed. Dieting is harder for them, but they should persist and work hard to keep their weight within the normal range. Exercise is even more important for them than other people. And they have to learn to be weight-conscious all the time. Their health and happiness depends on it. It is important for this small group of people to remember that while they are "predisposed" to be overweight, they are not "doomed" to be.

5. *I eat very little, but I keep gaining weight. Why is that?*

As we grow older, we need less and less food. Starting at about 38 to 40, every woman should cut down on food, because your body just does not burn it up as fast as it did when you were younger. The difference between a slim and an increasingly matronly figure may be just one piece of buttered toast every morning or two teaspoons of sugar in your cup of tea every afternoon.

If you are gaining on the same food intake that you have been used to all your life, keep a diet diary for two to four weeks. Find out just how many calories you are taking in. Weigh yourself two or three times a week to find out just how fast you are gaining—and then regulate your diet accordingly. Most women will have to do this every ten years after the age of 40. Studies have shown that after the age of 40 our caloric needs diminish five to ten percent every decade.

6. *Why should I diet? I know I'm fat, but I'm happy. My husband likes me the way I am.*

Recently an organization was set up to reduce discrimination against fat people. It's true that fatties are discriminated against. It is harder to get a job if you are too fat. If you do have a job, you may be paid less than a thin person. If you look at the men and women who have made it to the top executive level, there's hardly a fat one among them.

It is also true that women who are overweight are more likely to have varicose veins, diabetes, heart disease, gallbladder problems, arthritis, and hernias than women who weigh within the normal range. They also have more headaches, are more tired, more nervous and suffer from insomnia more than women of normal weight. They do not live as long as normal-weight women.

And they are less attractive.

My feeling is that if a woman is being discriminated against for being fat, and if being fat is bad for her, then instead of working to reduce the discrimination, she should go to work to reduce herself.

And her husband will like her even more because she has shown that she cares about herself.

7. *How thin should a woman be? I've always been a little stocky, even when I was a girl.*

A society woman is supposed to have quipped that a woman can never be too rich or too thin. And I don't think anyone has ever complained about being too rich. But there are women who have starved themselves to the danger point to achieve a fashionably thin figure—and that's ridiculous. Don't be brainwashed by the fashion magazines. Work out the most desirable weight for yourself based on your height and frame and age, and accept that goal as your natural weight. Learn to live with your shape, even if it is not as stringbeany as a fashion model's. There are all kinds of beauty, but the chief reason for dieting is health, and there is only one kind of health that is desirable—good health. So use your own good sense about how thin you want to be.

8. *Isn't it a good idea to tell your family and friends you are going to go on a diet so that they will help you stay on it?*

Absolutely not. It's just about the worst idea for a dieter. In the name of love, your friends and family (particularly the ones with no weight problem) will sabotage your diet. They will tell you that you look marvelous just as you are. That they don't understand why you are going on a diet.

They will make you try a piece of this and a taste of that. "It's so good," they will say, "just have one bite. It won't hurt you." Well, for some people there is no such thing as one bite. One bite leads to another.

Don't ask your husband to be your conscience, either. He will believe that you mean what you say, but every time he reminds you that some tidbit is not on your diet, you are going to resent it. The time will come when you will snap at him, "All right, all right, leave me alone." But if he does leave you alone, you will resent it even more. "Why did you let me order dessert? How could you let me go off my diet like that?" Asking your husband to be your conscience just sets up a lot of unnecessary stress in your marriage.

The woman who starts a diet by putting the responsibility on someone else is not planning to stick to that diet. Oh, she may think she is, but deep down inside, she is setting it up so that she will have someone to blame for her failure.

There is one exception: It can be helpful to confide in another dieter. That is one reason why Weight Watchers is so successful. When a group has a common motivation, they can offer each other a lot of meaningful support. So if you have a friend or relative who wants to diet along with you, you will probably be able to help each other.

9. *What about smoking? Won't you gain weight if you stop?*

The answer to the first question is "Don't." Smoking is bad for you. That's your life that's going up in smoke.

As to the second question, it used to be thought that giving up cigarettes almost automatically meant you would gain from 10 to 15 pounds. But new studies show that this is not true. The National Heart and Lung Institute did a landmark study on people who stopped smoking. The average weight gain was only 3.7 pounds. They also found that the better educated the person and the higher social class the person belonged to, the less weight they gained. So a smart middle-class or upper-middle-class woman will probably not gain weight if she stops smoking. She's smart enough not to make up for tobacco deprivation by stuffing herself.

However, if you feel that giving up smoking and going on a diet is too much to take on at once, my advice is give up smoking first. It is even more dangerous than being overweight.

10. *Why do people make such a point of eating breakfast on a diet? I am never hungry in the morning. Isn't skipping breakfast a good way to diet?*

Skipping breakfast can be the death of a diet. When I'm asked this question, I usually quote Dr. Morton Glenn, chief of the Obesity Clinic at a New York City hospital and assistant professor of New York University Medical School. "Skipping breakfast," Dr. Glenn says, "does not save calories. Eating breakfast is the surest way to prevent hidden hunger. This is the hunger that builds up during the day— the hunger that is responsible for nibbling in the late afternoon. Keeping your blood sugar under control by spacing meals results in better ability to control eating sprees. A breakfast of 200 calories makes a lot more sense than an unnecessary 500-calorie nibble later in the day."

CHAPTER NINE

How I Swam
From New York to Princeton

One reason Milt and I moved into our present apartment was the Olympic-size swimming pool in the basement. But, as it turned out, we had lived there for six years and never so much as dipped a toe in the water. Now, suddenly, the pool seemed to have a lot to offer—not the least being the fact that swimming consumes 500 to 600 calories an hour (if you really go all out).

A marvelous exercise for women of any age—a friend of mine learned how to swim at 61—swimming uses every muscle in the body without building bulging biceps or knotty calves (and it does wonderful things for the bosom). It keeps you supple, slims your waistline and tightens up the body. I was sure it would cure my sagging buttocks. Did they *really* sag? Or was I just imagining it? I was not going to ask Milt. If they *really* did, I didn't want to know.

If I could swim an hour a day, four times a week, and work off 500 calories each time, I could eat a maintenance diet—1700 calories—on those days and still lose weight. It sounded like something for nothing.

It was not. I had to work at it. But it paid off. Even when I came home dropping-dead tired, if it was my day to go swimming, I would get myself down to the pool hating every second of it. But I would have hated myself even more if I hadn't gone. And once I was in the water, it was absolutely marvelous. The pool was heated and it just seemed to un-kink all the nerves that had tensed during the day. I always left the pool feeling better than when I had plunged in.

It would have been ideal to swim every day, but I had to think of my appearance. There is no bathing cap invented yet that keeps hair dry. And I had to look presentable on camera every day. Twice a week there was a hairdresser on the set, so the night before I could swim and not worry about my hair. She'd put me to rights in the morning. But the rest of the time, I had to calculate just how much time and energy I had. Would I have enough get-up-and-go left in me after swimming to put my hair up in rollers so it would dry properly?

The first day, I just barely managed two laps of the pool and was completely winded when I climbed out. Every day I made myself do a little more. One more lap if possible. Or one more length. Or, at least, a few more strokes. And it worked. I gradually built up my endurance.

The lifeguard told me that 70 laps of the pool was the equivalent of a mile, so I set that as my first goal. The evening I first swam a mile was a staggering triumph. And staggering was what I felt like as I climbed out of the pool and walked to the dressing room. I eventually worked up to two miles a session. And I felt marvelous. Another thing that made me feel marvelous was throwing away my old bathing suit with its little dressmaker skirt that concealed the bulges. It was too big for me! I bought a simple black tank suit with a white stripe down the side, which was very flattering. And in a couple of months, that, too, began to look baggy on me. The next suit, also a tank suit, was bright red—a color that is great for blondes and one I hadn't dared wear for years. When I wore that red suit, I felt like something special streaking back and forth across the pool.

I set up a new goal for myself, something to keep me swimming after the novelty had worn off, just as I set up my weight-loss goals and rewards to make use of the Goal Gradient Principle (see page 37). I decided to swim to Princeton—or at least the equivalent distance—where Lisa was going to college. I pinned a road map up on the wall of my study, marked the route—53 miles—with a red crayon, and every night when I came back from the pool I would measure off my progress on the map. It seemed to take forever to swim from our apartment on the Upper East Side of Manhattan across the Hudson River, but once I was able to swim 2 miles a night, everything seemed to go—excuse me—swimmingly. I inched down the highway bit by bit.

The night I reached Princeton, I burst into our bedroom where Milt was reading in bed and told him, "I just reached Princeton!"

"That's nice," he said, "say hello to Lisa for me," and went back to his book. But the next afternoon the doorbell rang, and there was a huge box full of yellow roses with a note, "To the only woman who ever swam from New York to Princeton."

Swimming mile after mile—even with the built-in goal gradient of reaching Princeton—got to be boring, so I practiced new strokes. I'd do the crawl for a few laps, then the breaststroke, the backstroke and the butterfly. I'd even dog paddle for a few minutes. I had a really good time just fooling around in the water perfecting my strokes.

Another thing that helped keep me interested was a swimmer's watch that John Weitz, the men's wear designer, gave me. It was waterproof and had a little knob one could turn to mark each lap. I looked forward to completing a lap so I could register it on the watch. Another trick was to put a box of pebbles at one end of the pool. At the end of each lap, I would pick up a pebble and swim to the other end of the pool and drop it in an empty box. When I had transferred all the pebbles, my daily stint was finished. I don't know what the other people in our apartment house thought when they met me in the elevator in my white terrycloth robe, my hair plastered to my head and a box of pebbles under my arm!

It is not too pleasant to swim on a full stomach, but the only practical time for me to get down to the pool was after dinner, so that provided an additional incentive to go easy on eating at night—something I was able to do once I learned the trick of eating slowly. Milt told me that the old rule about waiting an hour after eating was nonsense and not to pay any attention to it, so as soon as I would get the kitchen cleaned up after dinner, I'd take the elevator down to the pool. By the time I finished and came upstairs again, it was almost time to drink my bedtime glass of milk and crawl into bed. I never had to worry about sleeping. After swimming, once my head hit the pillow that was it until morning.

And it was all worthwhile. By the time I treated myself to that red tank suit my body was in as good a shape as it had been when I was 20. My stomach was flat, my breasts were firm. That slight upper-arm flabbiness had disappeared and my buttocks no longer drooped—if they ever really had.

After I lost the 20 pounds, I tapered off on the swimming. Little by little, I put other things first until six weeks went by without my getting down to the pool. Then

I noticed that the flab was creeping back. I also did not feel as full of energy and bounce as I had when I was swimming. I decided to put the pool back in my schedule.

I was chagrined to discover that after only six weeks, I had slipped way back. I could only do fourteen laps. I got my lung capacity and staying power back fairly fast, but then I had to go away on a lecture tour and that put an end to the swimming for a few weeks.

By this time, I had become an exercise nut. I had learned how marvelous it made me feel—and look. I regretted the time I had to spend traveling across country to Los Angeles to appear on television specials and crisscrossing the country on lecture tours. I wanted to keep on exercising on a regular basis.

I suppose I could have continued with swimming. Almost every motel these days has a swimming pool, but when I'm on a lecture tour I feel I owe it to my audience to look my best—and I just don't look my best with my hair sopping wet—or with an emergency hairdo achieved with electric curlers. It is just not the same thing. And when you don't feel that you look your best, you don't act your best. So swimming out of town was out—no matter how enticing the motel pool.

Some women have a whole series of exercises that they can do anywhere there is space to lie down. Situps, leg lifts, bends, stomach rocking, shoulder stands, headstands. These offer an excellent workout—they are all fine and good for you, but I just don't enjoy doing them. And my idea of exercise, just like my idea of dieting, is that it has to be fun if it's going to work.

Then I found *the* exercise for me. One Saturday afternoon when Milt was watching the football game, they showed some film between halves of how the players trained—and there was this enormous brawny man jumping rope.

"That's it!" I thought. "I can jump rope any place."

Well, almost any place. One does have to be a bit careful. One early evening—it was in Cleveland—I was jumping away merrily in my hotel room at about five in the afternoon. I had a speaking engagement that evening and had decided to get my exercise early, then take a bath, lie down for a few minutes and dress—knowing that I would then arrive absolutely glowing. That's what jumping rope does for you.

Then the telephone rang.

"Dr. Brothers," the front desk inquired very cautiously, "do you have a child in your room?"

"No," I said.

"The guest in the room below you," the man at the front desk said, "has complained that there is someone jumping in your room. I told him, 'Oh, no, you must be mistaken. Dr. Joyce Brothers is registered in that room,' but he insisted."

I said, "Please tell the gentleman that there is no child jumping in my room."

I couldn't bring myself to confess that I was jumping rope. And that was the end of my exercise for the day. That's one reason why I like motels so much. There is no one downstairs.

Finding a jump rope was not as easy as one might think. I went out and bought a child's jump rope at the five-and-ten. It was just the right length for me, but a horrible rope. Plastic and much too stiff and light. I don't know how any child could have enjoyed jumping with that rope. Then I went to the hardware store and bought a length of clothesline, but clothesline must have changed since I was little. It got all twisted and was not a bit satisfactory. Then I asked my husband to find out what kind of rope they used in the gym where he plays squash. It turned out that they bought their ropes at a sporting goods store. And that's where I found the perfect jump rope. Stiff, but not too stiff, it has handles that swivel and it's just the right weight. So if you plan to take up jumping rope, the sporting goods store is the place to go for your rope.

It turned out to be the perfect traveling exercise for me. The rope tucks into the corner of my suitcase and it's always there. Sometimes I have to push the furniture around in the room to get enough space, but that's not too much of a chore. When I travel I try to jump at least ten minutes a day. That burns up about 100 calories, and is a really good workout. You get sweaty and your pores open and your face glows and your blood starts circulating and your lungs work hard. No matter how tired I may be or how little sleep I may have had, I never have to go out looking pale or tired as long as I can find a few minutes to jump rope.

When I was little, jumping rope was my idea of heaven. It seems to me that I spent most of my afternoons after school jumping rope on the sidewalk in front of our house. And even now, in my forties, I find it good fun.

It is therapy, too. This works two ways. When I arrive at a hotel after a long plane trip, it helps me feel better just pulling out the rope and skipping happily to some of the same rhymes I chanted when I was eight years old. One that is particularly ridiculous that I find myself using is, "One, two, three, O'Leary/ My name is not Mary/ If you think that's contrary/ Look it up in the dictionary."

Another is, "Shirley Temple is a star/ S-T-A-R/ Shirley Temple will go far/ 1 2 3 4 5 6 7 . . ."

And sometimes I make up my own jumping rhymes, like one evening after I had appeared on a panel television show with a particularly unpleasant man (I won't say who he is, but I'll give you a hint: he wears a toupee) , I went back to my hotel, pulled out my jump rope and began skipping away to this nasty chant: "1, 2, 3, 4/ Mr. X is an awful bore/ 5, 6, 7, 8/ He's a man who's easy to hate /9, 10, 11, 12/ In fact I wish he'd go to helve."

Silly? Yes. But the combination of hard, sweaty exercise and the silly spiteful rhyme got me over being angry and I went to bed in a very cheery mood.

It is impossible to overestimate the value of exercise. Not only does it help work off bad temper, it is the world's best tranquilizer—and does away with the need for sleeping pills. It is even more effective than an apple a day in keeping the doctor away. Most cardiologists agree that if a woman exercises vigorously for half an hour three times a week or more, it could make all the difference between having and not having heart trouble. This is why it is so important to start an exercise program the minute you are 40 if you have not already started one. As women enter the premenopausal and menopausal years, they lose much of their hormonal protection against heart attacks. Exercise will keep blood vessels elastic and build up circulation.

One doctor says that exercise is the closest thing to an anti-aging pill that is available. One reason for this is that our muscles, unlike other parts of the body, can be "rejuvenated." Exercise gives them tone and makes them stronger. It is possible for a 50-year old woman who exercises consistently to have better muscles than when she was 16. It is definitely true that the woman who exercises consistently— and exercises until she sweats—will be limber and supple when her contemporaries are beginning to walk around stiff-jointedly. Exercise counteracts many of the effects of arthritis and keeps arthritic joints mobile.

If there really is a Fountain of Youth, it probably is the sweat that pours off us during hard exercise.

CHAPTER TEN

The Sneaky Approach to Exercise

Much as I am convinced of the glowing benefits of exercise, there is no one more boring than the woman who insists on telling you about her gym class, her tennis game or the number of miles she walks each day. My approach to exercise is the same as my approach to dieting. Do it—and shut up about it. If people think you are naturally slim and trim, why spoil it by telling them you work hard to look that way?

Until now no one except my husband and daughter knew about the miles I swam in the pool. And you can believe that I did not tell the world that I jumped rope in my motel room every morning and night when I was out of town. But my sneakiest exercise is my telephone workout. I have a whole routine that sends Milt and Lisa into fits of laughter when they catch me at it, but I take it seriously.

When I am on the telephone, I start by bending forward from the hips and bouncing up and down like a limp rag doll, letting the hand that is not holding the telephone hang down. After a few bounces, I straighten up, take a deep breath, pull in my stomach, tighten my buttocks and then repeat my bouncing, holding the telephone in the other hand.

After that I straighten up, let one arm hang by my side and bend to that side seeing how far down my leg my hand will reach. I bounce sideways a few times, then straighten up and repeat on the other side.

If the conversation is still going on, I raise my elbows, place my hands on my shoulders, getting the telephone hand as close to my shoulder as I can, and bend backward from the waist, bouncing back three or four times. Then I switch the phone to my other hand and repeat.

If it's a really long conversation and I'm dressed for it, I then do a few kneebends. If not, I simply stand and lift one knee and then the other as high as I can. I continue this slow-motion running in place until I hang up.

It may look ridiculous, but it is an extremely efficient way of getting a little extra exercise that limbers me up—and burns up a few more calories.

Another sneak exercise that will burn up seven and a half calories a minute is simply stepping up and down one step as fast as you can. Try to do 30 steps a minute—and don't try to do more than a minute at first. This is an amazingly good exercise. It's a good warmer-upper, too. When we are at our sprawling, chilly old farmhouse in the country, I spend a minute stepping up and down the first step of the kitchen staircase to get my blood circulating after I've been working at my typewriter at the kitchen table.

If your telephone is located near your stairs, you can alternate my bending and stretching workout with stepping on long conversations. A friend of mine in New York City who lives in an apartment without any stairs taped some old telephone books together (the New York book is very thick) to make a step for herself. Another substitute might be one of those concrete construction blocks or a very sturdy wooden box.

When I talk about exercise there is always one woman who will say, "I can't do that sort of thing. I can barely touch my toes. And I'm too old to start a routine of situps and kneebends and headstands."

Not true. No woman in average good health is too old to start an exercise routine until—oh, maybe, her early nineties. I'm serious. Every woman should be able to touch her toes. Can you? If not, make this your first goal—but watch your back! Don't force yourself. The standard kneebend and twists and toe-touchings that have become associated with the "daily dozen" are not the only ways to limber up. And there is absolutely no reason for a woman to force herself into this kind of routine unless she finds it enjoyable. There are hundreds of other ways of limbering up that will help you reach the toe-touching goal without that daily-dozen routine, and I will suggest a number of them in this chapter. But if you have never done these standard exercises, don't dismiss them out of hand. Done under skilled supervision, they will help you exercise every part of your body, and many women find them fun. That's why the exercise classes in New York, Chicago, Los Angeles, and other big cities usually have waiting lists. Women from 20 to 70 pay to join in an hour of directed exercise. Friends of mine swear by their classes. They are as loyal to them as they are to their hairdresser or their most comfortable pair of shoes. One woman, a department store executive, has gone to the same exercise studio five times a week for the past 15 years—and you should see her. She is over 50 and you would swear she is no more than 35.

If you cannot afford an exercise class or live where they are not available, check out the Y, the local adult education center, and watch the ads in the paper. Almost every community offers yoga or modern dance or beginners' ballet if not plain old exercise classes—and they are all magnificent body shapers and calorie burners. There are also television exercise programs. And the women's magazines offer exercise programs just about every other month. So if this appeals to you, there is plenty of variety and opportunity around; something for every budget.

The woman who is fortunate enough to enjoy this kind of exercise has a true lifetime investment. She can always do these exercises. They require no special equipment and take very little time. The 67-year-old mother of a friend of mine, a woman who is still extremely active in church affairs and other volunteer work, does a series of exercises every morning of her life to a count of 100. This gives her an opportunity to vary the routine and keep it from being boring. Some mornings she touches her toes ten times and does five kneebends, twenty leg swings, ten situps and fifty jogs in place. Other mornings, she may omit all these and do another series. And she looks marvelous.

But if this kind of exercise turns you off, forget about it. There are other solutions. One of the easiest and sneakiest of exercises is walking. My parents are a living example of the great benefits of walking. They are healthy and chipper as crickets, both are still practicing law and—unless there is driving rain or snow—they walk back and forth to the office every day. A five-mile round trip.

A good brisk walk, the kind that covers a mile in 15 minutes, burns up 60 to 75 calories in those 15 minutes—as much as 300 and even more in an hour. A slower pace burns up proportionately fewer. But this is the most flexible kind of exercise there is.

Almost anyone can make time during the day to walk one mile at an all-out pace. And it is usually easy to find ways to walk as much as three or four miles a day without disrupting your routine too much. Take window-shopping (that's why I call walking a sneaky exercise), it's possible to walk for miles without even noticing it when you're going from dazzling store window to dazzling store window. Admittedly, this is an exercise better pursued in large cities with a goodly supply of show windows. But museum-going is also exercise, so is taking the kids to the zoo.

And one particular form of walking that I heartily encourage is the walk with a purpose, which helps broaden the horizons of the woman of 40, while narrowing her beam. These walks include bird watching, star watching, insect collecting, wild flower collecting or simply noting down varieties of scarce species. This kind of walking opens the mind and usually brings the walker into touch with other people with fresh interests—and that's a very necessary stimulus for all of us.

I'll give you two examples. The first is my neighbor Karen who indulged in what may have been the sneakiest approach to exercise ever. She bought a beautiful, thoroughbred Newfoundland. Buffy was six months old when he came to live with Karen—and seemed as big as a young bear. Buffy had to be walked—three to five miles every day. As a result, Karen began losing one to two pounds a week without making any change in her eating pattern. She found that having to walk every day no matter what the weather made her feel better, gave her more energy and definitely improved her figure. But before you follow Karen's example, be sure you really love dogs. A dog is a responsibility and an expense. But he's also a marvelous exercise taskmaster. He won't let you forget that he has to go out. And you'd better not ignore his reminders. Or else.

Another woman, the wife of a business associate, came to me for advice. I'll call her Cynthia.

"I know you don't accept patients," she said, "but I do need advice from someone I trust. My husband has made some remarks about how great a figure I used to have and how sparkling I used to be. That sort of thing. Then he always ends up talking about how I just don't have the energy and bounce I used to have. I see the writing on the wall.

"I've gained weight," Cynthia said. "About thirty pounds, a pound for every year we've been married. And every once in a while I'm surprised when I catch sight of myself to see that thick, middle-aged figure. But I'm no good at getting up in the morning and exercising. And I find it very hard to stick to a diet. But I'm ashamed of myself. Ashamed of the way I look. Ashamed of my lack of willpower. And I'm scared my husband might start looking somewhere else."

I reassured her. "No, I don't think he's going to look anywhere else. He's very fond of you."

"That's it," she cried. "Fond! He used to be in love with me. Now I'm like the fat old tabby cat that he scratches behind the ears every now and again. I'd like to pull myself together—without telling him what I'm doing in case I fail—but I don't know how to go about it."

Cynthia was shy. Now that her children were grown, her interests had narrowed rather than expanded, and she really did look matronly and dowdy. She looked older than her husband.

"Well, the best way to get started," I told her, "is to start on something that interests you, something you want to do, something that will provide you with stimulation. Does that give you any ideas?"

Fortunately, it did. Cynthia told me that she had always wanted to learn how to paint and that occasionally when no one was looking she used to sit out on the porch with her sketch pad and make drawings of a great old tree on the lawn and of flowers.

"Marvelous," I said. "Now you've got to get yourself off the porch. Take your sketch pad and your box of paints and walk someplace every day and don't come home until you have done a watercolor."

"Is that all?" Cynthia asked dubiously. "That doesn't seem like enough to get me pulled together."

"You have to make a start," I said, "and every time you make a change, even the smallest change, other things start to change. So try this and tell me how it works out."

I didn't see Cynthia again for months, then we met at a cocktail party. She looked very well. She had lost weight, changed her hairstyle and was more vivacious than I had ever seen her.

"You look very well," I said.

"Yes, I think I do," she agreed, "and I've been meaning to call you and thank you. You were so right about the importance of making a change. Can I tell you about it?"

When I said yes, she told me how she had gone out, bought herself a new sketch pad, some new watercolors and some pastels, and then walked out to find subjects to paint.

"I started going to the most isolated places," she told me, "because I couldn't bear the thought of anyone looking over my shoulder and seeing how terrible I was. And I really was terrible. But I didn't care. I kept thinking that at least I was getting out of the house, getting some exercise and doing something that made me concentrate very hard.

"I got so interested after a few weeks," she said, "that I looked around for an art class. I found one that seemed right for me at the Y. And it was. Everyone was as bad as I was. Then I made friends with a man in the class and told him about how I had been going out for walks finding scenes to paint. He asked if he could go along, too.

"This was nice, having someone on my own level to paint with and talk about painting. We talked about all sorts of things as a matter of fact when we were walking. It turned out that he was retired and was doing something he had always wanted to do—learn to paint. Having his company gave me a lot of courage. I didn't worry about people peering over my shoulder any more. We used to suggest locales to paint to each other, and would end up walking miles to find just the right place. I never thought of this as exercising and I was always surprised at how the time flew.

"My husband liked my new friend and enjoyed chatting with him when he'd stop for a drink after our painting excursions. My husband also began to remark how well I looked from spending so much time outdoors. And I really did look better. And I had lost weight.

"The best thing," she said with great satisfaction, "was that it got me out of my rut. I started buying new clothes—good-looking pants with heavy ski sweaters to go painting in. And as I got thinner, I bought more clothes to wear at home—warm, feminine things. All of a sudden I realized my image was changing. My husband began introducing me as 'My wife, the painter.' He showed off some of my better pictures. And we sort of entered into a new phase of life together."

"You're not afraid that he's going to 'look elsewhere' now, are you?" I asked.

"Not a bit," she laughed. "He's keeping his eye on me these days. And I like it."

I was very impressed when she told me her story. I was not surprised, however, because I have seen time and time again how just one change triggers a whole new life-style. In fact, my diet and exercise efforts did the same thing for me.

The lesson is that you just have to get up off your rear

end and do something. And sitting, incidentally, is death on the hipline, but if you must sit to watch television, do try to do something else—knitting, sewing, rotating your ankles. And use the commercials to burn up calories, not to eat. I sometimes jump rope during commercials or bicycle away on my exercise bike (and you don't have to invest in a whole exercise bicycle, there are stands you can get to attach to your regular bike).

Of course, real bicycling outdoors is a far better exercise than pedaling away in front of the television set and if you can bicycle six miles an hour, which isn't terribly demanding, you'll burn up about 250 calories in a very enjoyable manner.

An absolutely delightful exercise that falls into the sneaky category is ballroom dancing (these days the kids call it touch dancing). This gives you and your husband or any other man you are on dancing terms with, the opportunity to dress up, get out of the house, hear some light music and stay on your toes all evening. And if you feel like making love when you get home—and it's quite likely that you will—then you will really have had an evening's good exercise. This is an extra sneaky exercise, because you are also getting the man in your life to exercise (he probably needs it) without his suspecting that either of you are indulging in calisthenics.

I particularly like to go dancing—partly because I will never forget how Milt and I learned to dance. Both of us grew up in families that had difficulty in making ends meet. On top of that, both of us were extremely ambitious, hard-working students. When Milt returned from World War II, he wasn't inclined to be frivolous; all he wanted to do was finish college and get into medical school. And I had been terribly busy carrying two majors. When we got engaged, we decided that we wanted a big wedding, something that we would remember all our lives. We made lists and lists of guests. We discussed the menu for the wedding dinner by the hour. We compared prices of all the small orchestras that played at weddings—and we suddenly realized that neither one of us knew how to dance! Not a step! We had to learn how. At that point, Arthur Murray was offering a special deal to two couples who came in for instructions together. So my mother and father and Milt and I went to Arthur Murray's and afterward, at home, we would practice what we had learned.

At the wedding reception, we all stepped out in style. Milt twirled me into the middle of the floor with the opening waltz. My parents followed. And everyone was impressed with our facility and grace—or so we thought.

After the wedding, Milt and I had no money to go dancing. The only chance we had to practice our new skill was at the weddings of our friends. And then—rock and roll came in. Our Arthur Murray lessons had not prepared us to cope with this. And dancing became a thing of the past.

But now it's coming back. Our old wedding steps have put us in the forefront of touch-dancing fashion. Now Lisa and her friends ask us to teach them how to foxtrot, and Milt never fails to remark when we go dancing, "Well, I wish we had a few more investments that were still paying dividends twenty-five years later."

And don't forget about square dancing. This lively form of dancing burns up 350 calories an hour, and qualifies as vigorous exercise. It is also good for the woman alone who may not have an escort to take her dancing. Many communities have square dancing classes and it absolutely does not matter if you attend by yourself.

One important rule for sneaky exercisers of 40 and over is that "It's never too late." Many of us have always had a wistful desire to learn how to play tennis (420 calories an hour), or golf (300 calories an hour), ice-skate (360 an hour), fence (300 an hour), bowl (250), or ski (600 an hour, which doesn't mean the time you spend on the lift), but now that we have more time and more money don't start because we hate to look awkward or think our bodies are too old to master these new skills. This happens to be nonsense.

One of Milt's colleagues and his wife were in their middle forties when they took up skiing. For the first time in their lives they had the money and were able to take the time to indulge themselves. They were a bit timid about breaking bones and absolutely paranoid about appearing ridiculous, but they went ahead anyway. They made reservations at a Vermont resort and enrolled in the "baby" class at the ski school. And they loved it!

Today they are in their fifties and are madder than ever about skiing. No, they don't do the daredevil trails. They prefer cross-country skiing to up-the-lift-and-down-the-slope skiing. They pack a lunch and ski through the beautiful snow country, coming back to the lodge late in the afternoon when the shadows begin to lengthen across the snow. "We expect to ski for the rest of our lives," they say.

And the woman who swims, plays tennis or engages in almost any other sport can expect to do the same thing. Tennis is also one of those sports that people think they are too old to learn at 40 or over, but this just isn't so. The secret is in getting good instruction, starting slowly and building up your endurance little by little. You're not out to play tournament tennis, but to enjoy yourself. And just to add to your enjoyment, remember that every minute you play you burn up seven calories. And tennis also keeps you involved with people, vigorous people.

Gardening is another wonderful form of exercise, but

only if you enjoy it; if it is just another chore, then for heaven's sake, don't consider it your exercise. You won't get enough out of it. But if it is the kind of thing you like to do—and I have just discovered that it is something I love to do—the bending, kneeling, pulling and pushing that is involved gives your whole body a workout and burns up 220 calories an hour.

I never suggest housework as the equivalent of exercise. Very few of us really enjoy it and in today's automated households, a woman only burns up about 180 calories an hour. And it's drudgery. I don't know any woman who rushes home for the sheer pleasure of getting out the vacuum cleaner or who looks forward to doing the ironing. We all appreciate the end product, but housework is just that—work.

Stairs are a marvelous sneaky form of exercise. When I go shopping in big department stores, I try to take the stairs instead of the elevators. When I do take an elevator and it is empty, I sneak in an exercise. I flatten my spine against the wall, pull in my stomach and stand as straight as I can. This helps you walk more erectly, which means you automatically look younger. It is a way of counteracting the forces of gravity that pull us all into careless posture. This same exercise is a good one to do at home or in the office two or three times a day.

I have been emphasizing the sneaky aspects of exercise, but if you really enjoy jogging or mowing the lawn or sawing wood, go ahead. Enjoyment is what counts. Just be sure that one way or another, you get in three sweaty exercise sessions a week as well as some sort of daily workout, whether it's simply running up and down stairs or leaping on a horse and galloping through the countryside. Whatever exercises fit your life-style and give you pleasure are the ones to pursue. And you'll never regret it.

CHAPTER ELEVEN

Artist at Work

Any woman can be her own Pygmalion, transforming herself into a work of art. With diet and exercise she can uncover the body that was hidden by flab and lazy muscles and allow the beautiful woman who has been hiding in that body to emerge.

Shaping up is only part of the job. Time is bound to leave its traces—and not all of them kind. Once you have reached your weight goal, you may feel a bit like a vintage Rolls-Royce. The lines are marvelous, the engine finely tuned, but it would be even more desirable with a little touching up—some paint and polish.

The choices open to women today go far beyond mere paint and polish. The woman who so desires has an almost limitless number of procedures for self-improvement at her disposal. And if you are a woman who so desires, I want to encourage you to go ahead and make the most of yourself. I have never believed in the theory that "This is the way God made you and this is the way you should stay." People used to say, "If God wanted people to fly, he'd have given them wings." Well, God did give people wings—but, thank goodness, He didn't attach them. And God or someone has provided a host of ways for modern women to remodel, restyle and rejuvenate themselves.

A word of warning: Don't get trapped in the futile pursuit of youth. You'll never catch up with it. And who would want to? If you think back and brush aside the curtain of romantic nostalgia, your youth was probably not all that happy. Mine was moderately happy, but let me assure you that my butterfly years are turning out to be absolutely blissful. The goal that we are working toward here is the ability to fulfill our truly amazing potential and make our "second lifetime" the truly best years of our lives. And appearance counts (I'll explain its vital importance in Chapter Fourteen, "The Importance of Being Beautiful"). So, how do you start?

A woman can have all sorts of plastic surgery from a face-lift to a fanny-lift. Buttock-sculpturing often leaves ugly scars, however, and I am also told that occasionally it interferes with "essential functions," so I would never advise a woman to go through this operation—and as you know, I'm the first to worry about droopy buttocks. But a face-lift. That is different. A face-lift can liberate a woman and open up a whole new life for her. It will definitely lop ten years off her looks.

Many women, sadly enough, seem to consider this cosmetic surgery a kind of cheating. When Nancy S., the school librarian, announced that she was going to spend her vacation getting a face-lift, one of the teachers smugly observed, "I've earned my face. I wouldn't consider letting a surgeon rob my face of character."

To tell the truth, neither would I, but I would certainly consider a face-lift. When my face is ready, I intend to have one. A skilled plastic surgeon can soften the ravages of age without taking away any character. No woman has "earned" sagging jowls, puffiness under the eyes, drooping eyelids, wrinkles, a crepey neck and all the rest. They are the result of the force of gravity and the wear and tear of life. There is no reason why we should not smooth and lift our faces just as we reupholster an expensive sofa—tightening its sagging springs, adding fresh padding where necessary and covering it with a beautiful new fabric.

If you have the money, there is no reason why you should not spend it on a face-lift if that is what you want, just as there is no reason why you should not remodel your kitchen if that is what you want. And if you don't have the money, there is nothing to say that you can't go out and earn it. I think banks should grant loans for this kind of self-improvement just as readily as they grant loans for home improvements such as remodeling the kitchen.

Many women who feel they would be happier and more successful if they looked a little younger and more attractive hesitate to have plastic surgery.

"I would feel guilty if I spent all that money on myself," one woman stated.

"Don't you think you're worth spending money on?" I asked.

This simple question startled her. She was silent for a moment and then said, "I suppose I am," as if she had discovered a great new truth. "It is just that I am so used to doing without so that the children and my husband can have what they need."

She stopped and thought. Then she started talking again. "Everyone in my family looks better and dresses better than I do. I look ten years older than my husband.

"I guess the trouble is that I don't know how to put myself first."

Too many women who are now in their late forties or fifties were brainwashed by society (and themselves) into thinking that once they got married, everybody else came first. They feel guilty when they spend significant time or money on themselves.

The glory of the second-chance years is that once a woman realizes this, she truly has a second chance—the equivalent of a whole second lifetime in which to arrange her life and set her priorities to suit herself. Putting oneself first is not selfish. It is a healthy manifestation of self-respect. There is a difference. The woman who does not respect herself will not be respected by others. It is as simple as that. This is the reality. So if you think a face-lift will make you feel better about yourself, go ahead and start planning for it. Don't just sit there and wrinkle.

It is only in the last ten to fifteen years that cosmetic surgery has been safely available to the average woman. There used to be an almost universal disdain not only for the "vain" woman who sought plastic surgery, but for the surgeon who "stooped" to do it. Today surgeons accept the idea that women have a right to look as well as they feel. As one eminent plastic surgeon told his colleagues, "Looking old and being old are two different things. Some faces age prematurely because of the rapid pace of our life." Now most doctors have accepted face-lifts, breast-lifts, eye-lifts, nose "jobs" and the rest as completely legitimate surgery. And about time.

The plastic surgeon cannot perform miracles. He will help you look about ten years younger, but he will not turn you into an Elizabeth Taylor or a Marilyn Monroe (and even Marilyn, I am told, needed a little cosmetic surgery to make the best of herself). Your face will still be your face with all its character intact, but it will be smoother and firmer, its outlines better defined. People who were not in on the secret will probably say something like, "Oh, you must have had a marvelous vacation! You look so rested!" But friends who knew what you were up to tend to express a little disappointment. "Well, you look fine," they will say, "but you don't really look different."

This is because they remember your face from ten to twenty years ago, not from last month.

Not every woman who wants a face-lift will be accepted by a plastic surgeon. The initial consultation is really a careful screening. Dr. Michael Gurgin explains this from the surgeon's point of view. "The mere fact that a patient asks for a face-lift and feels it will do her good," he says, "is not sufficient reason for undertaking the operation. It is the responsibility of the surgeon to evaluate the patient's motivation, her physical and emotional problems and how much the surgery will do for her."

Dr. Gurgin divides his patients into age groups—those under 45, those 45 to 55, and those over 55. "Women under forty-five seldom need a face-lift," he says, "and it generally does not do much good. But there are some who age prematurely and whose profession—like modeling or acting—demands that they look their best. For them, even a minimal amount of correction is worthwhile and should be available to them.

"The forty-five to fifty-five group is the largest. The woman looks in the mirror and dislikes the signs of aging. Or it may be a feeling of inadequacy, a feeling that she is losing her lover or mate to a younger woman. Widows and divorcees who must suddenly vie for men may seek surgery. Sometimes women must be helped for economic reasons— they must return to work after many years of absence. Today, business favors youth and these women are discriminated against when they seek jobs. They have every right to expect help."

Women over 55, says Dr. Gurgin, "generally just want to look better. Almost everyone shows signs of aging by this time. And they should be helped, because people generally feel better if they look better."

He recalled one woman who came to him, candidly admitting that she had had three face-lifts already. She was in her eighties. "But," he said, "she was very healthy, had an active social life and was anxious to look her best." He agreed to do the surgery and the results were good. When she left after her last checkup, she told him, "I'll see you again in five or ten years."

Surgery can turn the clock back, but it can't stop the clock. The aging process continues. However, you have gained ten years and, as Dr. Gurgin's elderly patient shows, there is no reason why most women cannot have a second lift—and a third. Except money. Cosmetic surgery costs a lot—from a minimum of $1,500 to an average of $3,000 to "the sky's the limit" for women who demand private rooms and private nurses.

And there are risks. Face-lifts come under the heading of major surgery, and there can always be problems. For this reason, it is important to be in good health, to have the best surgeon available and to have the operation performed at a large teaching hospital. I feel so strongly about this last precaution that I always advise women who do not live in or near large cities to arrange to go to New York or Los Angeles or Chicago or whatever large metropolitan center is nearest their home, so that they can be in a teaching hospital. Then in case of an emergency, the best medical care and specialists will be immediately available. It is your face and your body and you want the best for it. This is elective surgery and there is no emergency about it, so you have time to plan and save so that you can have the safest operation possible.

It is also rather difficult to find a good plastic surgeon. Most of the top ones practice in the large cities and are affiliated with the teaching hospitals. I tell women to ask their gynecologist, their internist and their dentist for recommendations. You can also ask the hospital where you would like to have the operation for recommendations. Another source is the American Academy of Facial, Plastic and Reconstructive Surgery. You can write to the Academy at 1110 North Main Street, Durham, North Carolina 27701, and ask them to recommend a surgeon in your area.

Once you have settled on your plastic surgeon, let me warn you not to expect tender loving care or a gentle bedside manner. Most of them tend to be cold and withdrawn rather than warm and reassuring. It has something to do with the surgical temperament. But you are not looking for coddling and flattery. What you want is skill and competence.

And don't forget, like all major surgery, it is going to hurt. The pain is nowhere near unbearable, but there is some. And most women suffer from a kind of postoperative depression. You may feel miserable and sad. Your head may ache and your wounds may hurt or itch and all you want to do is cry like a baby. But you can't. Tears are forbidden. They are bad for your face. Your hair is full of dried blood from the operation and your scalp itches—but you can't wash it, because that is forbidden, too. You have to sleep on your back so there will be no pressure on your raw new face or strain on the stitches. And when they take the bandages off, you look awful.

But after the first week, you feel much better. In two weeks, most women can go out in public. And in six weeks you will look a glowing ten years younger.

So there you are. It is expensive. It hurts. It takes time. And there are risks. Many women will never feel the need or desire for a face-lift, but if you do, and if you have faced the facts about this cosmetic surgery, then by all means, take advantage of what it can do for you.

And then there is orthodontia. It is no longer "kid stuff." More and more women are going to bed these nights with "night retainers" (if you are unfamiliar with the vocabulary of orthodontics, don't worry, night retainers are not moonlighting houseboys or butlers or gamekeepers) and some even sport "railroad tracks" by day as they resculpture their mouths with this newly fashionable tool.

I believe in orthodontia as firmly as I believe in plastic surgery. It can make a world of difference in your looks. I used to think that I was the oldest person in the world to go to the orthodontist. When I was a little girl, I had two protruding front teeth which gave me a distinct resemblance to a bunny rabbit. My folks thought I looked "cute" and saw no reason to do anything about those two front teeth, but the minute I was out of college and earning money of my own, this little bunny rabbit hopped off to the orthodontist. In fact, I hopped off to several, because the first two or three wanted to pull teeth in order to "make room" to straighten my front teeth. I was having none of that, and today most orthodontists agree with me. Pulling teeth as a way of cleaning up one's mouth is frowned on. So, if you think your teeth need realigning, take my advice and keep hopping until you find an orthodontist who says he can give you a better looking mouth without pulling teeth.

My teeth are still straight and in the proper position. Take a look at them the next time I'm on television. I'll try to remember to smile enough so that you can see for yourself. In fact, some people ask me who capped my teeth because they're so even. That's how good a job my orthodontist did.

Capping is another procedure a woman should consider. Once this was done almost exclusively for people in show business, but today it's for everyone. If your front teeth are wearing down unevenly; if the porcelain fillings seem to stand out like a sore thumb, then ask your dentist about capping your teeth. Caps look completely natural and you will have a prettier smile (see page 122 for the importance I place on a smile).

Another new dental tool, and a very exciting one, is tooth implantation. This is for women who would rather die than wear dentures. And it costs. A woman could have four or five face-lifts for the money she would invest in a total implantation. Implantation is a surgical procedure in which false teeth are implanted one by one in your jaw. For some women, one or two or three of these implants are sufficient so that they will have something to anchor a bridge on. And this, of course, is not so expensive. But one woman I know, a retired realtor who is in her sixties, had her complete mouth done. It took six months to finish the job and she suffered almost incredible pain on four or five of her visits to the dental surgeon, but she claims it was worth it. It cost her more than $10,000, so at this point it is not for everyone. I am sure, however, that as this exciting new procedure is done more and more the prices will come down—and the doctors may be able to implant with less pain to the patient.

There seems to be no age limit on this operation. My own dentist told me that a 77-year-old patient of his had four front teeth implanted. He tried to talk her out of it, explaining how very painful and costly it was, but she insisted. "I love to go swimming at Cape Cod in the summer with my grandchildren," she told him, "and I am always worried that my dentures might fall out in the surf. I'd hate to have the children see me absolutely toothless." My dentist said, "She felt strongly about this, so I went ahead—with good results. She is eighty-two now and the implants are as sturdy as you could ask for."

And I understand that the sister of the Shah of Iran

visited an American dental surgeon for this procedure. So you can understand its appeal to women of all races and economic brackets.

There are other beauty tools women should consider as they get into their fifties. Electrolysis, for instance. The hormonal changes of menopause sometimes stimulate the growth of facial hair. It may be a few coarse hairs sprouting from the chin or a fairly heavy growth on the cheeks. For these women electrolysis is a blessing. It is not particularly painful, particularly risky or particularly dangerous. You have to go to a skilled electrologist. I would prefer to have this done by a dermatologist—and some of them will do it. If you can't find a dermatologist who is willing to do it, then at least go to an electrologist who is highly recommended by a dermatologist. This is important because in some states electrologists are not licensed and there is no control over them.

The simple hairstyles of today could not be more favorable for the woman over 40. A good cut is more important than weekly trips to the hairdresser. As one stylist told me, "Hairdos are out of fashion. The woman whose hair is set and teased and combed out is the woman who looks older than her years. When a woman in her forties or fifties comes to me, I almost always advise her to do two things.

"First of all, I suggest she cut her hair. Long hair is attractive on youngsters, but it tends to make the mature woman look older than she is.

"My second suggestion is on color. Women tend to want to keep their hair the color it was when they were young. This is the most unflattering thing they can do. Their skin is no longer the color it was in their youth. So their darker hair looks harsh. It is aging. Nature is wise and most women should glory in their graying hair. It can be so flattering if it is properly cut and cared for. And a sprinkle of silvery gray is marvelous.

"On the other hand, if her hair has that harsh pepper-and-salt look, then I advise lightening it, little by little. Week after week, I help the woman become lighter and lighter and lighter. This way, the woman becomes accustomed to her new coloring and learns to adjust her cosmetics to it. Her friends seldom realize the extent of the change because it is so gradual. As the hair lightens, I streak it, but just slightly. And eventually, as the years go by, I suggest a woman shade her hair into an ash color that is ageless—and most becoming."

I asked him about the blue rinses and the reddish-brown hair that many women in their sixties affect. He shuddered. "Absolutely not. I would not let a client of mine do that to herself. So harsh! Those reddish-brown tones not only look amateurish, they give an unattractive yellowish tinge to aging skin. And the blues, well, barbarians used to paint their skin blue. I can't imagine why a woman would want to tint her hair blue. Insanity!"

There is no one way for a woman to look. The woman who is seeking a new image for her second-chance years should be as careful as if she were buying a great painting or a new house. After all, this is a work of art she is creating, the shell in which she is going to live out her life. I tell women who ask me for advice to try on wigs to see how they look in different styles and colors. It is well worth the money to go to a top hairdresser for a consultation. Study the fashion magazines carefully. And study the ads as well as the fashion pages. Advertisers pay hairdressers fabulous sums to style the model's hair in these ads, so they are well worth your attention. Accumulate a file of hairstyles that appeal to you so that when you do go to the hairdresser for a consultation, you can show him or her what you like and the colors that appeal to you. He may talk you out of them, but this means that he will have to give you reasons why this look or that color is not suitable for you. And that is an education in itself.

There is more to the wonderful world of color for women. Even the color of one's eyes can be changed if you feel that would add to your general well-being. Contact lenses these days are far more sophisticated than they used to be—and much more comfortable. Dustin Hoffman and Dame Judith Anderson, both of whom have blue eyes, turned brown-eyed to lend conviction to their roles as Indians in one movie. Tinted lenses can give hazel eyes a greener tone or a topaz one, and can deepen faded blue eyes (you know that washed-out blue) to a beautiful and natural-looking deeper blue.

You have to be careful about makeup when you are wearing contacts. Most cosmetics have an oily base that can coat the lenses. Doctors caution against using powdered eyeshadow and the lash-extending kind of mascara when you are wearing contacts. When you are fitted for your lenses, ask your ophthalmologist just what cosmetics you can and cannot use.

I have left the fun part until last—finger painting. We women are lucky. We have the most wonderful canvas in the world to work on—our faces. Sometimes we get in a rut and streak on the same dab of the same lipstick and the same scrub of the same powder every day. That is a waste of your face.

Unless the woman of 40 has been very cosmetic-conscious, I always suggest that she throw out all her powders and paints and start fresh. Skin tones change, hair changes, the contours of your face change—and it is now time to adapt your cosmetics to your present look, not to the face you had twenty years ago.

Experimenting to find the right makeup is even more fun than searching for the best hairstyle. It's worth going to a top makeup artist for a consultation and a lesson, but there is also excellent advice to be had from the saleswomen at the cosmetic counters in large department stores. Most of them have been trained by the firm whose products they are selling, so they can give customers advice on color and application. Many of them will give you a complimentary makeup when you buy cosmetics. And almost all will show you how to use any given product. Many cosmetic houses sponsor makeup clinics or offer special services during the year. Watch your newspapers for these. They are terrific values. And don't forget the women's magazines. Most of them devote several pages an issue to beauty and makeup, in which detailed instructions are given, usually accompanied by diagrams or full-color photographs.

While you are experimenting, my suggestion is to buy your cosmetics at the five-and-ten until you find out just what is most becoming to you. If you remember, I bought some silver eyeshadow as my first reward when I reached my first 3-pound goal on the diet. It was a disappointing mistake. The silver was too light. It accented the crepiness of my eyelids and was not at all flattering. I mentioned this to the head of a model agency—a woman who had been a model herself when she was younger and who is still remarkably beautiful. "Oh, Joyce," she said, "you should know better. As we get on, we have to stay away from those lighter shades. The browns and foggy grays, the darker blues and the olive greens are more flattering."

Then she took a critical look at me and said, "You

know, I think you really should tone down your makeup now. That pink and white look of yours is making you look older."

I was indignant. "I've always been pink and white," I said. "That porcelain look is the best for my skin and coloring."

"Do me a favor," she said. "Let me show you something." She sat me down, scrubbed off my makeup and pulled out a huge cosmetics kit that any makeup artist would be proud to own. When she was finished, I was amazed. I looked younger and prettier. She had used a soft beige foundation that made my skin look softer. And an apricot blusher instead of my usual pink. And she had done my eyes with brown and taupe shadow and just a flick of mascara. The look was subtle, fresh and flattering.

"As you grow older," she explained, "you should try for a healthy outdoor look instead of the delicate pink and white. This is an easier look for blondes."

When I went back to the television studio, I showed my new face to the makeup man and asked, "What do you think?"

He smiled. "It's marvelous."

I made one other change in my makeup. I switched to organic cosmetics. They seem to be easier on my skin. And the colors are really glorious. At the television studio, the makeup people were reluctant to use them at first. "They won't stand up under the lights," they complained. But I insisted. And they did. I looked rosy and glowing and young on screen. Or younger, at any rate. The colors do not last as long. That's true. But one can always take three minutes for a fresh makeup, if necessary.

Now I plan to keep on experimenting—trying different looks for evening and seeing what paint job is best for me.

And that's what it is—a paint job, and fun. It is your face and it is up to you to paint it pretty. If you make a mistake, there is always soap and water and you can start afresh.

There are other ways of gilding the lily. I'm sure you will find the ones that are right for you. And there are also some truly miraculous beautifiers that keep women looking marvelous and cost nothing—or practically nothing. I'll discuss these in the following chapter and if you don't take advantage of them, well, someone should spank you—preferably someone who loves you.

CHAPTER TWELVE

Free and Beautiful

It is almost true that "the best things in life are free."
The very best beauty aids are diet, exercise, the right kind
of sleep, clean skin—and a smile.

By now you know how I feel about diet and exercise,
but sleep is the third ingredient for health and beauty, and
one that is not fully appreciated. Getting the right amount
of good sleep is increasingly difficult as we grow older.
There comes a day when you suddenly realize that you are
not sleeping as well as you used to, that you can't fall
asleep with the television on any more and wake up rested.
This did not happen from one night to the next. It creeps
up on you until some pre-dawn you find yourself lying
there worrying that you will look and feel terrible the next
day because you're not sleeping and wondering how in the
world you ever developed insomnia. Relax, you probably
don't have real insomnia, which is an abnormal inability
to sleep.

As we get older, we need less sleep. Remember those
stories of how Winston Churchill slept only four or five
hours at night? Sir Winston, who was in his prime during
the wartime years when he symbolized courage and democ-
racy, could not have gotten along on that amount of sleep
when he was younger. But as his sleep needs diminished

with age, he adapted to his new sleep pattern and made the most of the extra waking time.

The important thing is that the sleep you get be good-quality sleep. That can be difficult, but there are many ways to court that deep, restorative, beautifying sleep. First, you have to accept that you need less sleep. It is quite simple to find out just how much sleep you do need. Make this test for a week. Take the clock out of the bedroom and make sure that the windows are heavily curtained so that the morning light won't waken you, then go to bed when you feel sleepy and get up when you wake. Make a note of the hours you have slept. Over a week, you will have a good idea of your true sleep needs—probably less than you thought. As you adjust your schedule to the sleep pattern you have established, you may find you are tired during the day. There is no law against taking a nap. If you are a working woman and an afternoon nap is impractical, try a short nap after you get home from work.

A busy executive in her fifties takes a bath every evening as soon as she gets home, then lies down for half an hour to read or sleep. After that, she says, she is ready for the evening. This short lie-down time makes all the difference for her between dragging around until it's time to go to bed and having the energy to pursue whatever she feels like doing.

If you have trouble falling asleep, I could not recommend that trusty glass of milk highly enough. The amino acid in the milk converts to a chemical compound that has a tranquilizing effect.

Another effective sleep-inducer is a bit of noise. If you have a clock radio, turn it on softly after adjusting it to turn itself off in case—just in case—you fall asleep. Some people find music sends them off to sleep immediately; others find music stimulating and swear by the drone of the voices on all-night news programs. There is also a machine that emits what they call "white noise." Psychologists and psychoanalysts whose offices are in new buildings with thin partitions often use these noise machines so that patients in the waiting room cannot hear what is being said in their inner offices. But their gentle hum has an almost hypnotic, sleep-inducing effect. There are more expensive models that reproduce the sound of rain or of waves and surf for people who feel these are extra soothing. One woman whose husband is at work on the Great American Novel every night, says that the sound of his typewriter puts her to sleep. So experiment until you find the noise that makes you sleepiest.

The woman who exercises during the day will have less trouble falling asleep. Exercise not only relaxes the body, but tranquilizes the mind. Studies have shown that many people who complain of anxiety or are diagnosed as being depressed tend to become calmer and sleep better when they follow a consistent exercise program.

I have found a couple of tricks to help me fall asleep when I'm away from home, as I so often am. I always take my own pillow. It's quite soft and flat, so it is no bother to pack. Somehow, sleeping on my familiar pillow makes it easier for me to fall asleep in a strange bed. Another thing I do is call Milt after I'm in bed and just about ready for sleep. We chat about what we have done during the day and that puts me in a very pleasant, comfortable mood that makes it easier to sleep. If I discover that I am lying there unable to doze off, I make up fantasies for myself. I think of things that I would like to happen and then I pretend that they have. A little like telling yourself a bedtime story —and it works.

The other problem we face as we get older is waking up in the middle of the night and not being able to get back to sleep. When Lisa was a baby, I was awake at her every whimper, leaping out of bed to make sure she was all right—and then I would fall back to sleep almost instantly. I can't do that these nights. When I do find myself unable to get back to sleep, I crawl out of bed, get into my warmest robe and go read in the living room. Sometimes I will have another half glass of milk. Warning: There is always a temptation to raid the refrigerator when you're awake in the middle of the night. Don't! If you are absolutely starving and feel that you could sleep only if you had a little something to eat, have a glass of warm milk and a piece of dry toast. You'll be surprised how much you'll appreciate the flavor of that toast with nothing on it, but don't turn into a night-eater. That is one of the easiest ways to get fat. The important thing is not to worry about being awake. If you don't sleep well one night, you will make up for it the following night.

Don't take a sleeping pill—unless your doctor *insists* that you do. They often perpetuate the problem. You get to feeling that you cannot get a good night's sleep without a sleeping pill. They also tend to leave you with a dull hangover kind of feeling the next day; you don't wake up refreshed the way you do when you've had natural sleep. So don't badger your doctor for a prescription. You are much better off without these drugs. Remember, you can trust your body. When it needs sleep, it will get it.

And then there is the matter of how you sleep. Most women alternate between sleeping curled up on their side or flat out on their stomach. I met a spectacularly beautiful woman in Rome a few years ago who told me that her most important beauty secret was sleeping on her back. Without a pillow. When she was young her grandmother told her that when women slept on their stomachs or sides, pressing their faces into the pillow, they were encouraging wrinkles, putting unnecessary pressure on the face and often stretching the skin. Lying on one's back, her grandmother told her, gave nature a chance to help her face. The force of gravity allowed the facial skin to relax and there was no pressure put on any area.

It may have been an old grandmother's tale, but this woman was in her late forties and her face was smooth and practically unlined. She did have those laugh wrinkles most happy women get.

There was one drawback to her beauty regime, she confided to me. Sleeping on her back made her snore. So she and her husband had had separate bedrooms all their married life. As a good Italian wife, she always started the night off in her husband's bed, then when he had fallen asleep she went to her own room, closed the door and went to sleep on her back—snoring peacefully.

My own sleeping beauty secret is an occasional 36 hours in bed. It does wonders. Every once in a while when Milt is out of town—usually about every four or five months—I spend from seven o'clock Friday evening until seven o'clock Sunday morning in bed. I start off with a long, luxurious bath, wash my hair and dry it, but I don't put it up, get into my favorite pajamas and get into bed. I always have a stack of paperbacks beside the bed. The radio is on my bedside table along with the paperbacks. The television set is at the foot of the bed and the refrigerator is stocked with skim milk, fruit, cottage cheese and eggs and yogurt—all kinds of healthy, easy-to-eat foods that don't need preparation. And I just stay in bed. On Saturday, I take another long bath and change my pajamas and crawl right back in bed. I sleep and wake and sleep and wake and don't worry about whether I'm awake in the middle of the night or asleep in the middle of the day. I just relax and do nothing. When I get up on Sunday morning, I feel marvelous and I look pretty good, too. This kind of time in bed is a marvelous escape from tension and stimulation, both of which we need, but both of which can get to be too much.

Another beauty aid that costs nothing—or next to nothing—is cleanliness. Many women are just plain dirty. And there is no excuse for it. There is no excuse for a dirty neck, dirty, dandruffy hair, for dirty nails, for hairy legs. There is no excuse for body odor. I am aware that some young women feel that unshaven legs, a gamey smell, lank and oily hair are an expression of liberation. I disagree. These women are isolating themselves from society—just the opposite of liberation. This lack of respect for one's body reflects a more serious lack of respect for one's self. Women who find virtue in being dirty should examine their feelings very carefully and as honestly as they can. Lack of care for one's body is a generally accepted sign of emotional disturbance.

The woman who cares about herself will bathe daily, use a deodorant and pay scrupulous attention to the cleanliness of her genital area (these odors tend to get somewhat rank with age). We are not aware of our own odors because our sense organs adapt to it, just the way most women are not really conscious of their wedding ring after they have been married for some time. It is only when they take that ring off that they notice it. Its absence is unaccustomed, therefore it is noticed.

I did not mean to turn this into a lecture on hygiene, but I have heard too many sad stories of women in their forties and fifties being turned down for jobs for which they were qualified—*because they were dirty!* Don't let carelessness, laziness, time pressures get you into the habit of thinking you're "clean enough." There is no such state as "clean enough." Either you are clean—or you are dirty.

A woman may be scrupulous about bathing and maintaining her body at its sweetest smelling, but still have a dirty face. The very best advice I can give to women from 40 to 100 who want to look beautiful is—wash your face with soap and water. I can hear the objections now. "I have not used soap on my face since I was fourteen," one woman will say. "Oh, I wouldn't dream of using soap. It's so drying. I just cream my face," says another. And so it goes. What this chorus tells me is that ninety-eight percent of American women are going around with dirty faces and looking older and less attractive than they should.

I mean it. Wash your face. You'll thank me for this advice. But don't just grab your washcloth and scrub away. In the first place, don't use a washcloth unless you will use a clean one for each face wash. That's important. Otherwise, use your hands. They are easier to keep clean.

Your best bet is a mild, unscented soap. There are many on the market from inexpensive to expensive and they all do about the same job. Wet your face, get it soapy, rub it gently and then rinse, rinse, rinse. Pat it dry. Some expensive beauty regimes urge following this soaping with a cleansing lotion to get the last traces of soap off your skin. That is a good idea, but I do something even better. The reason that there may be soapy traces on your skin, no matter how diligently you rinsed, is because most water is hard. If you use soft water, the soap comes right off and your skin is left smoothly clean. I found a small gadget that I attach to my bathroom sink that softens the water in that sink and I use that to wash my face with and to shampoo with. I never have any soap residue. Let me warn you that doctors have discovered that soft water is bad for you when you drink it, the sodium in it may be conducive to hypertension and other such diseases. Soft water is for exterior use only.

After you pat your face dry, it may feel rather tight and drawn. This is what moisturizers are for. Almost any kind is effective, from Vaseline to the moisturizer with a famous cosmetic name on it. This wash, rinse and moisturize routine is the one recommended by dermatologists who are concerned about keeping skins as young and smooth as possible for as long as possible. The proof of their wisdom is in front of us every day. Did you ever examine a man's skin closely? Think what he does to his skin in shaving once or twice a day. He lathers it up, he scrapes it, he splashes on aftershave lotion and the fact is that men's skin stays youthful looking far longer than most women's. They keep it clean and the dead cells are scraped off with the shaving. If you will check the skin of men who wear beards, skin that does not get this daily care, you will notice that these men have more skin problems (little pimples and blackheads) and that their skin is not as glowing and youthful as that of smooth-shaven men.

One of my personal beauty aids is still rather controversial and for that reason, I do not recommend it. It is vitamin E. Scientists have learned that this vitamin is necessary, but they have not learned how much of it is necessary—and they are not even sure what it is necessary for. Most doctors do not approve of women taking more than 10 or 15 units of vitamin E a day, because, unlike vitamin C, it is stored in the body and it is not known what the effect of a large store of vitamin E will do. But there has been so much talk about it that I take 200 units a day—for a very special reason. Some people call it the "sex" vitamin and I suspect that it does add to one's sheer physical energy. Others claim that it is good for the skin, but what convinced me to start my 200-unit dosage were the reports of findings by two research physiologists at the University of California. They found that vitamin E evidently encourages cell division (this is one step toward learning the secrets of living longer), but they point out, "We can't reverse the other important aging processes in the body, so vitamin E will not extend human life except in the possible case where people are subjected to severe environmental pollution."

As far as I am concerned, any woman who lives in a large city is subjected to severe environmental pollution. These same researchers went on to say, "Even if vitamin E can't turn a forty-year-old into a fourteen-year-old, it might prevent an early death or brain disease or heart attacks or senility." They added cautiously, "We say 'might.' Of course, we don't know these things for sure yet."

But what impressed me was that on the basis of their own research, these two scientists had started taking 200 units of vitamin E a day. And I started doing the same thing. If it doesn't make me sexier, or make me younger, at least it will give me a fighting chance against pollution.

But I repeat, this is a controversial vitamin. I do not recommend it for everyone. If you want to take the chance I am taking, consult your own doctor first. There may have been other findings on this vitamin between the time this book goes to press and you read it.

The final beauty aid—and one that I heartily recommend without a single reservation—does not cost a penny. Any woman who wants to look younger, more appealing and more beautiful should—Smile! This is the most effective beauty prescription around. It works. It really does.

CHAPTER THIRTEEN

"We Became Lovers Again"

What with dieting and exercising and my new cosmetics, I was looking better than I had for years. My skin had a glow, my eyes had a sparkle, and I felt very pleased with myself. I was getting used to people coming up and asking, "What have you been doing with yourself? You look marvelous."

I felt as if I carried a whole new atmosphere around with me—a lighter, more buoyant atmosphere. I began to walk differently. I was proud of my body. It was trim and slim and curvy. Unconsciously I developed a much sexier walk. I held my head higher. I was proud that the suspicion of a double chin had completely disappeared, and so had all the rolls of fat and flab that had distressed me.

Along with feeling sexier, I had more confidence in myself. Not that I have ever been a shrinking violet, but now I really relished making entrances, walking onto platforms, greeting audiences and meeting new people.

And I began to accumulate a whole new wardrobe. I truly felt like a butterfly emerging from her old cocoon. Those "safe" clothes, those good tweed skirts and little pastel jersey dresses and round-necked sweaters represented my old chrysalis and I was ready to discard it. Those daring chiffon pajamas had been the first step in my discovery of what I began to think of as the "joy of clothes." I wasn't the only one who felt the change. The stylist on the television show started bringing in completely different clothes—younger and sexier and brighter. When I wore them I felt very female. I stood better to show them off and I no longer had to be reminded to keep my legs out front. I loved wearing strippy high-heeled sandals that showed off my ankles, crazy platform shoes that added 5 inches to my height (the world looked different way up there), and boots.

Was this the *real* Joyce Brothers? The serious psychologist who always had a theory to fit every circumstance? Yes it was, and she was going to take some getting used to even for herself. I kept having relapses back to the old humdrum me, when I would protest, "Oh, I can't wear that. It's not my type of thing." And the stylist would insist, "Yes, it is. Just try it on and see. Now! Look in the mirror," she would say. And there I was. Was that me in that bare midriff at-home outfit? Yes, it was.

And the men on the show—well, they had always been more than kind. Comradely was probably the word to describe their attitude, but now they were looking at me twice. I was getting little pats and strokes that had never come my way before. And there were little acts of gallantry that even as a liberated woman I enjoyed tremendously. I don't mean that I had turned into Joyce Brothers, sex kitten. It was more Joyce Brothers, all woman. Everything combined to make me feel good about myself. As soon as I began thinking of myself as an "attractive dish,"—a phrase one of the crew had used—then I began acting like one.

My big breakthrough, the one thing that meant the most to me, came one night six or seven months after I had started my bit self-improvement program. We were getting dressed to go out and Milt said, "Why don't you wear that slithery pink thing. You look cute in that." I couldn't believe it. This was the first time in years and years and years that Milt had ever suggested I wear anything in particular. Oh, sometimes he would say, "Are you sure you're going to be warm enough in that?" But to suggest I wear "that slithery thing." Well!

I got a lot of compliments at the party on my dress. And Milt got a lot of compliments on me. Later, when we were getting ready for bed, he said, "Nick told me he had never seen you look better. He asked me, 'What's Joyce up to these days? She looks great.' "

"Oh, that's nice," I said. I could tell that Milt was really pleased. He was feeling the way he used to feel when we were courting and people asked him what a pretty girl like me saw in a struggling medical student like him and he would put on his smug look.

Then Milt said, "Well, what *are* you up to?"

If you can believe it, I blushed. And I said, "Nothing," like a guilty little girl.

That really got him interested. "What do you mean—nothing?" he asked.

I stammered around a bit and Milt lost his smile. Finally I blurted out, "Well, if you must know, I've been on a diet."

"Well, I know that," he said. "I've been watching you weigh dibs of this and dabs of that for your dinner for months now." He paused, "But what have you been up to?" he asked again.

Now I was relaxed. Of course he knew I'd been on a diet. "It's just that all the swimming and rope jumping and the diet make me feel just marvelous. Like I had a rampaging case of euphoria, if there's any such thing," I explained.

"I see," Milt said. "Well, hurry up and come to bed. Maybe it's catching."

I'm not saying that this was the actual conversation, but it is pretty close to verbatim, because I've played it over and over in my mind. It marked an important turning point in our marriage.

We became lovers again. And more.

CHAPTER FOURTEEN

The Importance of Being Beautiful

That old saying, "Beauty is only skin deep," is the most dreadful bit of nonsense—for women over 40. For the woman entering her second-chance years, beauty is a vital component of self-esteem.

There are fortunately as many kinds of beauty as there are women. I learned this years ago from a French psychologist, a man I greatly respected. We were talking about one of my colleagues in graduate school at Columbia. I remember telling him, "It's so sad about Julia. She is so nice, so bright. And such a good friend. But she just is not pretty. I'm afraid she will never get married."

He shook his head.

"No, Joyce," he said, "you're wrong. Prettiness is boring. Julia has beauty. It shines through her eyes. It is in her manner and the air with which she carries herself. To herself, she is beautiful. And so she will be to all those who are important in her life.

"And," the psychologist went on, "you have to remember that no matter how a woman looks to you, there will always be a man to whom she is beautiful."

That was before the Women's Movement, but his statement is still valid, still comforting, because women will always find happiness and satisfaction in the admiration of the opposite sex—and why not? Anything that bolsters our self-esteem is important; it is equally important to understand that there is always someone who responds to your particular beauty.

An American psychiatrist, Dr. John Schimel, Associate Director of the William Alanson White Institute, corroborated my French friend's statement. "There is no such thing as an ugly woman," he says. "Over the years I have treated women who were, for instance, extremely overweight and yet were extraordinarily attractive to certain men who pursued them vigorously."

This should not be taken as a license to allow oneself to be overweight. Being overweight is unhealthy physically and mentally. It really does affect the way one thinks of oneself.

"In the past year," said one woman who was part of a research project exploring how appearance and self-esteem were related, "I have lost 25 pounds, and I have gone from being a sort of cringing doormat to thinking of myself as a very worthwhile person whom people should feel privileged to be with. Perhaps the pendulum will swing back, but I'll never feel like such a dowdy little mouse again—unless I get fat again."

Women should be more aware, however, of the infinite varieties of beauty. Sometimes we underrate ourselves. One participant in a nationwide survey on body image said, "I had never met a man in my whole life who was not foaming at the mouth over big boobs. Not until I met my husband did I realize that a woman with small breasts can be considered sexy and attractive."

Beauty is far from a frivolous subject. In our society, if you don't look your best, forget it. The best jobs, the highest pay, the most interesting opportunities and—usually—the most desirable men go to the most attractive women. So it is vital that women learn to think of themselves as attractive and get rid of their one-track concepts of beauty. Just as that woman with small breasts learned that there are men who consider small breasts exciting, so women whose looks do not fall into the accepted contemporary beauty mold have to learn to consider themselves beautiful.

When I said this in a lecture, one woman jumped up and interrupted, "But what about me?" she asked. "And people like me? I'm no raving beauty and I never will be. You're saying that I don't have a chance."

I invited her to join me on the platform. She was somewhat overweight and looked heavier because she slouched. Her shoulders were rounded and her head poked forward. Her features were half-good, half-bad. Her nose was too big. But she had a wonderful smile.

"Here is a woman," I told the audience, "who feels that she is not beautiful. But she is.

"That smile of hers makes her beautiful. She should be conscious of it and learn how to use it just as one learns how to use a typewriter."

My platform guest smiled delightedly—and blushed.

"When you blush," I told her, "you look like a girl."

She blushed even more. And she did look like a girl, although I would have put her age at somewhere over 45 and under 55.

"You *are* beautiful," I said, "and you could be more so if you really cared." I paused, and then I went on, "I want you to care."

I turned to the audience, "Perhaps some of you feel you are not beautiful either?"

A nod and a hum of assent ran through the all-woman

audience like small waves washing from one side of the auditorium to the other.

"This woman's features are not perfect," I said, "but with a little help, the good ones can be accented and the bad ones minimized."

"It's my nose," the woman said. She had already gained confidence standing there and listening to me say she was beautiful. Now she smiled again and it lit up her face.

"Will you let me show the audience how beautiful you really are?" I asked.

She agreed and I left the platform to get my makeup kit from the dressing room. Then I sat her down with her back to the audience and did a sketchy "first-aid" makeup. I drew a white line down the center of her nose and blended dark foundation along the sides of her nose. I applied blusher to her cheekbones and put a little on her chin and forehead for good measure. This little bit of finger painting gave her that glowing color that she had had when she blushed.

Her own lipstick was just right—a reddish brown that added just the slightest bit of warm color, which is all most women over 45 need. Those bright lipstick colors are too harsh and aging for most of us.

I stood back and looked at her. "How can you say you're not beautiful? You look great."

And she did. But the makeup was only a minor role of her new look. The excitement and embarrassment of being on the platform made her eyes sparkle, her cheeks flush and generally made her look more alive. Stimulation may possibly be the greatest beautifier of all.* Certainly boredom is the biggest uglifier.

---

* This may be why so many lovers' quarrels end up in bed. As a woman gets angrier, her blood flows faster and she seems to vibrate and sparkle all over. She may put her hands on her hips and sway her

The most important component in this woman's new beautiful look was that she *felt* beautiful. As she turned to face the audience, they gasped as if a miracle had occurred. And, in a way, one had. My platform guest who had claimed she was no beauty was standing there simply glowing. Her slump had disappeared, her head was high.* There was color in her face, and that marvelous smile of hers was sheer magic.

The audience applauded. And as she walked down the steps from the platform, holding herself like a queen, I knew that this woman was never going to think of herself as a Plain Jane again. Why? Because she had been told that she was beautiful. And the statement had been reinforced by the audience reactions. Immediately she had started acting like a beauty.

Can one really become a beauty in just five minutes? Absolutely. I've heard of instance after instance of women who have experienced that one wonderful moment of truth when they realized they were beautiful. For some, it has been a visit to a hairdresser who convinced them to try

---

body as she tells off the man in her life—and at the same time she will thrust her bosom forward. All these sexually provocative signals— quite unconscious—that are triggered by the anger stimuli make her so attractive that her lover loses interest in the quarrel and becomes sexually stimulated. Since the woman's anger has already aroused her senses, she usually finds it easy to switch from verbal to sexual intercourse.

* There was no magic about her slump disappearing. Just before she turned to the audience, I had whispered, "When you stand up, stand straight and squeeze your buttocks." That buttock squeeze lined up her body, made her hipline smoother, forced her stomach and midriff in and helped her bone structure find its straightest erect line. This is an important little trick that every woman, particularly those who sit at a desk for long hours, should practice several times a day. Try it right now. Stand up straight, as erect as you can, and put your shoulders back. Now, squeeze your buttocks together. Feel the difference? This is great to counteract "fanny flab."

another hairstyle. For others, it has been a compliment that made them see themselves in a more desirable light. For still others, it has been a new dress.

One extremely successful saleswoman in a Fifth Avenue shop told me, "I learned very early that if I can make a woman feel beautiful, I have a customer for life. One day a drab-looking woman in her forties came into the dress department. I asked if I could help her, half expecting to hear that old put-off, 'I'm just looking, thanks.'

"But no. The woman said, 'Yes, I could use some help. I'm so heavy, I don't know what I can wear. Nothing looks good on me.'

"And certainly the suit she had on was most unbecoming. It accented her big rear end and had absolutely no style. She wasn't fat," the saleswoman said, "more pear-shaped. I had a number of outfits cut to flatter that shape. I brought a few into the dressing room for her to try on. One was particularly becoming.

"Suddenly this woman was standing up straighter and smiling at herself in the mirror. She fished in her pocketbook and pulled out her comb and lipstick. It was an almost instant transformation. She was obviously pleased and delighted with herself.

"She has been a steady customer ever since. She told me once that that dress had marked a turn-around point in her life. It had made her realize that she did not have to look middle-aged and dowdy. And she really succeeded. She now has an elegant style all her own. She looks much better in her fifties than she did ten or eleven years ago when she first wandered in looking for a new look—or at least a new dress."

As that saleswoman's customer proved, beauty is as much a state of mind as anything else. In our society where most people take you at your own value, it is important for the woman over 40 to achieve that state of mind. If you feel unattractive, people will consider you unattractive. If you feel beautiful, that is how others will see you.

Some women have told me that they just don't have a beauty potential. They refuse to be convinced that they can be beautiful. I tell them to study the attractive women they see in the movies and on television. Very few of them are classically beautiful. Most have flaws, some have very serious flaws, but all have made the most of themselves.

Take a look at Audrey Hepburn who is as emaciatedly thin in her forties as she ever was as a young European dance student. She is still skin and bones, her features are sharp, her body contours are equally sharp, but one accepts her as a beauty. She carries herself like one. And she has made the very most of her good points—those enormous, beautiful eyes.

Or look at Ingrid Bergman, 59 as I write this. One would never call her thin. Statuesque would be a more apt description. Her face is square. Her waist has thickened. But she is beautiful, and not the least of her beauty is that wonderful smile. The fact that her hair is graying, that the lines are beginning to show and that she is no longer reed-slim do not matter. She acts beautiful—and she is.

Then there is Barbra Streisand. I remember when she was an unprepossessing, overweight singer. Today, she has a slim elegance, a chic that is completely her own. Her nose? Yes, it is big. But it is part of her beauty. She has made herself into an individual with her own look. And that look is beautiful.

None of these women are girls, but they are all as beautiful or more beautiful than they were when they were younger. And there are hundreds of others like them, women who are accepted by the public as beautiful. Some are too thin, others too fat. Some have bad figures, others bad complexions. But they have all learned to make the most of themselves.

There have been a number of significant studies in recent years on the importance of being beautiful, those scientists who poke into how we behave and why have discovered that looks are not only one of the most important ingredients of a healthy self-esteem, but that they also affect the way others react to us.

A rather impudent bit of research done by a writer friend of mine illustrates this point very nicely. Over 40 herself, she was working on an article about male and female attitudes toward women based on appearance. When she heard that there was an opening for an assistant to work for two women editors on a large magazine and that the applicants were to be interviewed separately by both editors, she decided to embark on her own research project. She applied for the job.

When my friend went to her first interview, she was carefully groomed. She wore a smart outfit by a name designer and walked into the office with a big smile and an air of self-assurance, obviously looking forward to the interview. She was very direct and explained that she did not have much experience, but that her children were now old enough to take care of themselves after school, that she was anxious to get back into the working world—and that she was sure she could handle the job.

On the second interview with the other editor, she wore an old raincoat over a nondescript sweater and skirt. She tied a kerchief around her head and dabbed on a bright lipstick that made her look rather haggard. She hesitated as she walked into the office and looked a bit frightened. This time she claimed to have had a lot of experience.

When the two editors compared notes on applicants, one said, "I saw a Mrs. X today. She's just what we're looking for. Not much experience unfortunately, but I have the feeling that she will learn fast. And she's eager."

"Great," said the other woman. "I saw a Mrs. Y. And she was impossible. Her background was okay, but I wouldn't want her around the office."

They asked Mrs. X to come back for a final interview. When she walked in, both editors were there. She explained what she had done and apologized for wasting their time. After some initial indignation, the editors decided it was pretty funny and agreed to talk about the basis on which they chose Mrs. X, who had no experience, over Mrs. Y, who was well qualified. It was, of course, on the basis of her appearance and her air of self-assurance.

This informal "ministudy" is quite revealing. It shows that women seem to be swayed by how other women look—just as much as men are. There have been other studies along these lines, quite important ones and—naturally—much more scientifically conceived and carried out, but they all corroborated what my writer friend discovered in her own audacious ministudy.

The findings of all these studies add up to the fact that it is really not so much how you look, as how you feel about yourself and your looks that matters. For instance, fifty percent of the women taking part in one study said that they considered themselves attractive. This same group also rated higher in self-esteem than the women who did not consider themselves especially attractive. Another study revealed that women who feel that they are good-looking also consider themselves to be more intelligent, more conscientious, more forthright—and more downright lovable than other women.

I cannot emphasize enough just how much confidence in your looks gives you confidence in yourself. Until I was about 40, I was scared to death of talking to people I didn't know. I felt self-conscious and stiff. I had absolutely no command of small talk. In front of an audience or a class of students or with someone who was asking my advice, I was all right. I felt sure of myself and my subject. But put me in a purely social situation—and my hands would get clammy.

Then after that "confrontation" with myself on the television screen that I reported at the beginning of this book, the day that started me on my big self-improvement campaign, this began to change. As I lost weight and changed my image, I began to feel more attractive and surer of myself, and this was reflected in the way I walked and talked and in the clothes I wore. It's a bit like boiling a lobster, you know. You put it in a pot of cold water and you turn the heat on and little by little it gets boiled and doesn't even know it. That's what happened to me with clothes. Little by little I started wearing more flamboyant colors, sexier dresses that clung to my figure and moved with me. Then I started moving with them. It was all different. I just wasn't the same. I felt sexier and more interesting—well, I am sure I looked more interesting.

Researchers have also discovered that a woman's self-esteem is very closely related not only to her feeling attractive, but also to being thin—and I can testify to that from my own experience. After I had lost those 20 pounds, I was more conscious of my body. It was easier for me to relax in front of the television cameras. I felt myself loosening up—using my hips and shoulders, letting my hand trail along the back of the sofa or the side of the table, as I walked to give my body a longer more graceful line. Earlier, I would have been quite self-conscious about that kind of thing, but now I was so pleased with the way I looked, I really wanted to show off on the television screen. I found myself smoothing skirts down over my hips with both hands in an almost unconscious gesture that called attention not only to my new slim waistline but to the rounded curve of my hips. And you would never catch me hiding my legs under a chair anymore. They were right out front. And I was not above indulging in a bit of ankle twirling or doing a few dance steps to make the most of a favorite long skirt I had with high slits up the sides.

The day came when I took a belly dance lesson on screen and suddenly realized how far I had come. There I was rotating my hips as suggestively as I could, my knees were no longer "locked together" as Johnny Carson used to tease me, and my bosom was rotating in its own rhythm. When Milt saw that show, he said, "I'd like to have that film for my private collection." I told him, "That's ridiculous. Why settle for a picture when you can have the real thing?"

Beautiful women have an advantage all their lives. Even when their beauty fades, their self-esteem stays high.

There is only one significant exception—the extraordinarily beautiful woman. When a woman is so beautiful that everyone remarks on it, this can *weaken* her self-esteem or even prevent her from ever acquiring it. She thinks that people only value her because of her beauty, and she knows that she had nothing to do with her looks— she was born with them. Studies have shown that the great beauties tend to become unhappy in their forties and grow progressively unhappier. They had thought that their beauty was their reason for existence, identity enough. And when it begins to fade, they are lost.

All of us who have had to work to make the most of ourselves so that we can start our second-chance years with the dice loaded in our favor can take comfort in knowing that women who were born beautiful have to work even harder adjusting to life after 40. All too often they spend what should be their butterfly years shriveling up into unhappy old women. Many of them fall into one or the other of the categories illustrated by my friends Robin and Alicia.

Robin was a popular model, but a few years ago, in her early forties, she went into business as a dress designer.

"For the first time in my life," Robin told me, "I feel happy. I am accomplishing something. Before, I always felt that it was my looks people admired. I kept peering in the mirror every day after my fortieth birthday, looking for signs of age—and finding them. The more I found, the worse I felt. When I was no longer beautiful, I would be nothing. It was a terrible feeling." She looked ready to cry as we talked.

"But you are still beautiful," I said, "and you always will be."

"Perhaps," Robin agreed, "but it doesn't matter. Now I feel much better about myself. I know I have achieved something.

"Being beautiful can be a minus, not a plus," she said earnestly, "because you always worry that you are nothing but a face and figure."

Robin meant every word of it.

My other friend, Alicia, a rich New Yorker, is quite the opposite. She was the "beauty of the year" when she made her debut. Today she is in her middle forties, has been married (and divorced) three times, spends several weeks a year at a Swiss clinic devoted to maintaining the youthful appearance of wealthy women, and looks as if she were in her late fifties.

"I don't know what to do," she said. "How do you do it? You look younger than I do. And we're the same age. What's your secret? What do you take?"

"Take?" I asked. "Not a thing. Just my vitamins. But I

work at keeping my weight down and get plenty of exercise. I guess my only secret is hard work.

"I really do work hard," I told Alicia. "I write and lecture and do a lot of reading to keep up to date with new developments in the field of psychology. And I run our household. A woman comes in to clean, but I do all the shopping and cooking. And now that Milt and I have bought that old farm, I spend a lot of time up on stepladders painting or down on my knees stripping old coats of varnish off the floors."

"I don't believe it," Alicia said. "With all that work, you should be exhausted."

"No," I said. "Work is what keeps me going. I'm interested in everything I do."

"If you say so," Alicia said, "but there's nothing I can do. I don't have anyone to cook for. No children. No husband. I don't even know how to play bridge."

I suggested a number of ways for Alicia to make her life more interesting, but she did not want to be helped. She had spent her whole life being admired for her beauty, and she was as addicted to that admiration as an addict to a drug. Unfortunately, because she drank too much, smoked too much (women who smoke wrinkle more and earlier), lay in the sun too much and felt sorry for herself too much, her beauty was only a memory. Alicia was no longer a ravishing young girl or a ripely attractive woman. She looked older than she was.

Fortunately, most women improve with age. *Women's Wear Daily,* the bible of the fashion industry, once ran a series of pictures of prominent women as they were and as they had been ten years before. They included famous models, well-known fashion designers, women in politics and business, actresses and socialites. In every case, these women looked more attractive "now" than "then." They radiated assurance, energy, good health and the beauty that comes from relishing life. Each woman was active. "What magic have these women put to work?" the newspaper asked. And then supplied the answer: "In most cases a better understanding of their physical types has resulted in improved good looks." That understanding just had to involve work to keep what they had and to achieve the remarkable improvement each woman showed as she became older. The discipline of exercise and diet, the willingness to experiment and learn—these were the basic ingredients of their new enduring beauty.

The woman who works to change her appearance, to get and stay thin, to look as beautiful as she can will be rewarded with an extra dividend: a new sexiness. One psychiatrist says, "Changing one's appearance so that one *looks* sexy and confident can change one's image of oneself enough so that a woman plays the part in a better sex performance—and sexual success keeps breeding sexual success." This scientist says that just as during your school days, when the teacher informed you that "neatness counts" in a written examination, it is equally true that "looks count" in sexual enjoyment. And isn't it nice that we have learned there is a man to appreciate the very particular and individual charms of every woman? It is even nicer as one enters the second-chance years if that man is your very own husband. Not that I'm knocking lovers, but there is something wonderful in rediscovering the exciting world of sex with the man who has shared your life for so long.

The woman who cares enough about herself to make sure that she embarks on her butterfly years looking her most beautiful will find a very special dividend in the renewed attention and ardor of her spouse. It happened to me. And it has happened to many other women.

In an earlier chapter, I described that blessed blindness that besets husbands so that you always look to him like the girl he married ten, twenty, twenty-five or more years ago. To him, you are the same slim, beguiling charmer. So if you tell me that you are going to tint your hair, he will probably say, "Oh, why do you want to do that?" And he'll mean it. He quite literally may not see the gray—at least, not on a conscious level. And if you tell him that you are going on a diet, he will probably say, "Oh, why do you want to do that? You look fine to me." Or he may say something like, "I like a woman with a little meat on her."

But the fact is that you can make any number of changes in yourself without your husband really consciously noting them—as long as you keep your mouth shut. You can gradually tint your graying hair or streak it. You can re-sculpture your figure. You can do almost anything except turn into a redhead overnight and he won't really notice it. But one day, he is going to see someone else looking at you with an interested eye, or he's going to hear someone say, "Your wife really looks great these days," and suddenly he will look at you with fresh eyes. His psychic eyesight has been sharpened and he is going to see you as you are today, not as you used to be. And he's going to like what he sees—a lot.

What causes this? It is simply that his inner censor has relaxed. He realizes that you look marvelous the way you are right now. He no longer has to cling to his memories of you as a bride. He no longer has to suppress the reality of how you look in order to justify his own good judgment in choosing you to share his life. He no longer has to close his eyes to what may have been an encroaching dowdiness in order to protect himself from the knowledge that he himself was reaching middle age.

And when this inner censor relaxes and lets him see and

appreciate the new beautiful you, it is like having another woman in his life. It is *very* exciting. When this happens, there is a kind of second honeymoon, a rekindling of sexual interest. Now he starts spinning new sexual fantasies about you, the new woman in his life. You become excitingly desirable again, not the familiar bed partner. And your sex life becomes—beautiful.

CHAPTER FIFTEEN

The Truth About Sex

One night some months after our twenty-fifth wedding anniversary, my whole sexual relationship with Milt changed. It went from good enough to marvelous. Or on a scale of 1 to 10, I would say it went from 4 to 10+ (see Chapter Thirteen, "We Became Lovers Again"). I have no intention of going into the details of our sex life except to make it clear that it is everything that I had ever fantasized it could be. And the big change came in my late forties.

The trigger for the new relationship was Milt's suddenly seeing me as I was, a woman who had changed and grown in the twenty-five years since we were married, a woman who was still attractive—and more than that, attractive to other men. This provided a whole new stimulus for him. And his fresh interest provided a whole new stimulus for me.

Other women have discovered a whole new dimension to their sex life in their forties and fifties. This usually takes the form of a new freedom.

"I never realized how inhibited our sex life had been until our youngest went off to college," an old friend told me. "Now we're like silly young kids again. We made love in front of the fireplace last weekend for the first time in twenty-three years! Can you imagine. There never was a time when we had that kind of privacy after the first child was born—and she arrived ten months after our honeymoon."

She laughed and said, "If only someone had told me how great it was going to be, I wouldn't have spent all that time worrying about the empty-nest syndrome. I'm delighted to have the kids out on their own. Oh, I love it when they come back to visit, but I'm ready for my own life now. And sex is something I intend to catch up with."

She stopped and then she said, "Guess what we do Saturday afternoons these days?"

I guessed. It was not hard. "You have wine with your lunch and spend the afternoon in bed."

"Right," she said. "And that's what we do Sunday afternoons, too. You know, sex is really too good to be wasted on teen-agers. They don't know how to enjoy it."

"I'm not sure I agree with you," I said, "but I do think that most of us lose sight of how marvelous sex can be in what I call the butterfly years. All the fun—and none of the responsibility."

"Yes," she agreed. "I can't believe how lucky I am. No more worrying about getting pregnant. No lying awake at night wondering if I'm going to get a stroke from the Pill or if there's a little rip in my diaphragm. None of that business of having to say, 'Just a minute until I go to the bathroom,' and then when you are putting in your diaphragm one of the children wakes up and has to go to the bathroom or wants a drink, and by the time you get back to bed—your husband has fallen asleep. You know, I used to dread the menopause, but it's the greatest thing that ever happened to me."

"Yes," I agreed. "Between freedom from children and freedom from the fear of pregnancy, those are the years of the most blissful sexual experiences. The menopause is nothing but what my husband Milt refers to as a treatable disease and once it is under control (I'll discuss this in the next chapter), there is a new element of fun and sponta- neity. Or, at least there should be. Some people miss out on the renewed pleasures of sex, and this is a shame. The problem with many marriages (remember that cartoon with the fortyish wife looking at her husband and wonder- ing where the magic went?) is that we don't really under- stand what the magic of sex consists of. It is in your head, not between your legs. If this were only more clearly understood, there would not be so many men and women over 40 buying expensive how-to manuals and attempting one uncomfortable position after another. Some couples intent on recapturing earlier thrills conscientiously trans- fer their lovemaking to the floor or halfway up the stairs or, as in the case of one couple, to the windowsill. This last exercise turned out to be a mistake.

"There I was," the wife told me. "My buttocks on the windowsill, my head hanging down outside—and all of a sudden I saw our next-door neighbor looking up from his backyard. My upside-down view of him could not have been anywhere near as intriguing as his view of me. I begged Charles to quit. "Stop it," I hissed. "Help me up! Quick!" But he was coming and didn't even register what I was saying. As for me, all I felt was frantic embarrassment at what that nice suburban neighbor of ours must think at seeing me halfway out of our bedroom window on a sunny Sunday morning with my husband standing over me ener- getically pumping away. When Charles finished and real- ized we had an audience, he nearly let me fall out the window. The moment he helped me up, I went right downstairs, grabbed the real estate section from the Sun- day paper and started looking. We moved six weeks later.

"Our children could never understand why we moved. My son said, 'I thought you and dad planned to live in that house, or at least in that neighborhood, forever. All your friends are there. You belong to the country club. You've both worked on that garden for years and years. I can't get over your deciding to move.' And I just couldn't tell him what prompted our decision," she concluded glumly.

Not all unconventional positions and imaginative love-making lead to such drastic changes in one's life, but unless both of you are irresistibly seized by a desire to titillate the neighbors or accumulate black-and-blue marks, your own bed and bath offer all sorts of more comfortable pleasures. There is right side up and upside down and sideways, half on the bed, half off, there is hot and cold, standing and sitting; there is even being spread-eagled to the bedposts, if your mutual fancy so inclines (but don't use your good silk scarves; use his old neckties). And—off the bed, but still in the bedroom—an old-fashioned armless rocker offers tried and true satisfactions.

It is important to understand that few of the contortionist positions in the manuals lead to better sex. They are not really meant to. Their function is to stir up excitement in the hope that this will rekindle ardor and make sex breathtaking again. Unfortunately, they rarely work—for women, at least. There is nothing "wrong" with these positions. In my view there are no wrong sexual practices or postures *provided both participants find pleasure in them.* I mention this because all too often the older man, in an effort to stimulate his lagging (often sagging) organ, urges new and different positions on his partner—ones that may be either embarrassing or uncomfortable for her. And in that case, she can say goodbye to her orgasm. Unless a woman is strongly masochistic, she just is not going to enjoy sex that hurts or makes her uncomfortable. Too many women have been brainwashed into believing they are lacking because they don't feel comfortable making love while standing on their heads or hanging on to the top of a door while their hands grow numb, or because they find anal penetration painful. They are *not* lacking. Most women get the most pleasure out of intercourse in the "old-fashioned" positions. There is a reason why these positions are old. Sex isn't exactly new. And it didn't take too many centuries for women to discover what really felt good.

The way to put that old shivery excitement back in sex is to use your head. Learn what turns your husband on and tell him what turns you on.

One well-known actress recently asked if she could have a private talk with me. "I never thought I'd be complaining about not getting enough sex," she said. "I've always been the one who has told my husband, 'not tonight, I'm too tired' or 'I'm not in the mood,' but these days it's my husband who's making the excuses. He just doesn't have it any longer.

"When he gets hard, he has to get right in. And then it's one, two, and if I'm lucky, three thrusts—and that's that. It just doesn't do anything for me. I told him so the other night."

"Well, that may not have been wise," I said.

She had obviously expected sympathy, but what she had told me was more of a capsule sexual history shared by thousands of couples. The woman who in the earlier days discouraged her husband's sexual overtures, who resisted sex "on demand," discovers as the forties wear on into the fifties and the sixties that now she has to encourage her husband's attentions. There is both a physical and psychological reason for this. The woman over 40 is often far more vigorous than she used to be, while the man's energies are diminishing.* Then, to compensate for his flagging interest in sex, the man rather spitefully turns the tables on his wife to pay her back for all those spurned overtures. He is the one now who resists sex on demand. This is absolutely not on a conscious level. The man accused of this would deny it vehemently and self-righteously. And yet, psychiatrists have learned that this revenge is a very important component in men's sexual reluctance in the years after 50.

This need not be accepted as a permanent condition, fortunately. Sex is too strong an urge and too sweet an experience to be kept repressed for long. A woman who cares can easily interest her husband in sex again. The first step is to realize that neither he nor she can perform as they did when they were 18 or 25 or even 30. One thing that upsets men and often renders them temporarily impotent is the current myth that nothing about sex changes with the years and that for the normally virile man it is full steam ahead up to the age of 90. This is not true. Not for men. Not for women. One can have a most satisfactory

---

* An interesting indication of how early masculine sexual vigor begins to diminish is that adolescent boys and young men up to the age of about 25 have a "sex thought" *every other minute*. Men actually reach their sexual peak at 18 and after that it is all downhill. By the age of 25 the frequency of sex thoughts is less than half of what it was at 18. And by the time a man reaches 65, he does not think about sex more than once every ten minutes. This may still seem a rather high frequency to women, but remember, the thought is not father of the act. It takes more than a fleeting whim, idea or fantasy for the older man to "get it up." There are exceptions to these findings, of course. A man who is in his fairly vigorous forties or early fifties and who is extremely absorbed in his business or career may not even think of sex for three or four weeks at a time.

and delightful sex life up to the age of 90, but it is going to be different. Men do not have erections as easily and as often. The man who used to want sex five times in an evening becomes the man who can only manage an erection once every five days. The ejaculation also diminishes as the years go by. Women maintain far more sexual vigor, but even they suffer some diminishment. While women still enjoy orgasms, the contractions are not as vigorous as in earlier years. The woman who would have had five or six or possibly ten or twelve strong contractions at 35 will probably have only three or four at 70 and they will be weaker than those she enjoyed thirty-five years ago. But they will be good—and she still has the capability to enjoy multiple orgasms.

It is important to understand that this diminishing vigor is normal so that neither partner gets hung up trying to reach some unrealistic performance level just because they think everyone else functions at that level. Everyone else doesn't.

I explained all this to my actress friend and suggested that if she wanted to reactivate her sex life, she should spend some time thinking seriously about what turned her husband on. This takes work, you can't just bustle into the bedroom one night and say, "Things are going to be different from now on." I usually advise people to give themselves a vacation. Not the kind of vacation where you are seeing eight countries in ten days, and not the kind of vacation where the children are popping in and out, but the kind where you go to a pleasant resort hotel or take a cottage by yourselves for a week. Your chief activities may be walking on the beach, sitting by the pool, exploring the area. That leaves plenty of time for the two of you to explore each other, to reach a new sexual level easily without even thinking about it. It won't hurt to invest in something ravishing to wear to bed, or in a bottle of champagne. The emphasis should be on the four f's—fun, festivity, frivolity and (if you will allow me) fucking. But no pressures.

It is more important to keep in mind that as we get older, sex becomes more mutual. It is no longer something a man does to his wife or a woman does to her husband; it is something they do together. And even if their sex drive is disparate as they grow older, there are still occasions when they will be in perfect synchronization with each other. And when they are not, well then, there are many steps a woman can take to get the physical pleasure she craves.

For instance, she can embark on a love affair.

I have to admit that I have completely reversed my attitude toward extramarital affairs. In my previous book, *The Brothers' System of Liberated Love and Marriage,* I made it clear that I did not think marriage should be so liberated as to embrace extramarital affairs. I cited the case of 28-year-old Claudia, who consulted me because her husband just could not keep pace with her sexual demands. "I am always the one who suggests we go to bed," she said. "Dan is the one who makes the excuses. I get to feeling so frustrated, I'm thinking of taking a lover."

"What's wrong with a plain sex-for-sex's-sake relationship?" she asked. "I'd make sure it didn't spill over into my relationship with Dan. He'd never, never know about it or suspect it."

I told her flat out that that wasn't true. Psychologists are aware that when a woman is engaged in an affair and the husband does not realize it, it is simply because he refuses to realize it. It is next to impossible to keep a meaningful sex relationship secret. A woman has a different air about her, a secret smile. In her sexual life with her husband, there may be slightly different rhythms, gestures, caresses. There may be a different odor about the woman of her lover's body, or his cigar or his aftershave lotion. She may give it away in her conversation. The woman who has never been the slightest bit interested in automobiles for example, may suddenly start talking about fuel injection systems or the former "financial idiot" may start following the stock markets.

I also told Claudia that a love affair, instead of strengthening her marriage by keeping her sexually satisfied, might indeed weaken it. Just because the affair represented a change. Any change, as I explained earlier, has a ripple effect. The ripples may be slight, but they are relentless. Nothing can stop them. If there is a weak spot in the marriage, the ripples may destroy it.

"If you want to have an affair," I said, "it's your life. But are you willing to take the chance? To make the gamble that it won't affect your marriage?

"I don't think any woman has to tell her husband the absolute truth," I said, "about her every little thought or action. But by and large, truth makes for closeness. If a woman has an affair, there is forever after an area that she does not—and cannot—share with her husband. It is a walled away enclave that, like a nonmalignant growth, is always there and has the potential for turning malignant."

Claudia pondered this. "I don't want to risk my marriage," she said. "But I'd like more sex."

Eventually she solved her problem by masturbating—manually and with a vibrator. She had been shocked when I suggested it, but I advised her to discard her sexual rigidity. There is nothing wrong with masturbating.

She called me several weeks later and said, "You know, I wonder where I've been all my life? I guess I really did believe my mother when she told me I shouldn't 'touch myself down there.' But I'm a grown woman now and, you know, those masturbation orgasms are the best of all!"

I laughed and told her not to get too hung up on her friendly little vibrator, but I congratulated her on having coped with her sexual appetites without taking a chance on her marriage.

(Incidentally, women who feel too embarrassed to go into a store and ask for a vibrator should know that an electric toothbrush—without the brush, of course—is very effective. And some women swear by the Water Pik. It makes one wonder what dentists have been up to all these years.)

But that was several years ago, and my ideas have changed. Not about masturbation (I think it is a highly satisfying solution for many women, especially women who find themselves without a husband or steady sexual relationship in the years after 40), but about extramarital affairs. For some women an affair can add a little extra spice, a fresh dimension and a lot of magic to the marriage. As I say, I resisted the idea for a long time. I am very conservative about everything that relates to marriage and the family. My interest is in preserving these institutions, not weakening them. But as I travel around the country talking to women, I have come to the conclusion that there is a dividing line somewhere in the forties. On one side of it, an extramarital affair is downright dangerous and inadvisable; on the other side of that line, however, it may even strengthen a marriage.

An affair is not for every woman. Some women would feel it was wrong, sinful. For them, it *is* wrong. Others would feel uncomfortable, although tempted. For them, an affair is also inadvisable. But the woman who is strongly tempted and attracted to a man who is not her husband, gets my nod of approval—if she feels she can handle both the affair and her marriage.

It can be done. Liz had an affair with Sam, the husband of her best friend, which lasted for almost six months. "That was one of the most delicious periods of my life," Liz told me. "I enjoyed it immensely. I was a little girl with a secret. I was a woman with a lover. Life began to be very exciting.

"At the same time," she said, "my marriage was wonderful. Wonderful! Our sex life was better. There was a spark between us that had not existed for years."

The two couples had known each other since they were newlyweds living in the same apartment house. When Liz's husband turned 50, he and Sam decided to look for land in the country where both couples could build their dream houses for retirement years. One weekend, a real estate man called to offer ten acres with some frontage on a lake. Sam's wife had the flu. Liz's husband was out of town on business, so Liz and Sam drove out to look at the property. Afterwards, they had lunch at a famous country inn— and after lunch, they went straight upstairs to one of the bedrooms in that inn.

"We didn't have to say anything," Liz told me. "It just happened. And it was great. After that we tried everything we could think of to get a few hours together. It was always marvelous. Neither of us would have dreamed of breaking up our marriage. Not for a moment. I loved Al and I knew Sam loved Jane. We were simply coasting, loving the feeling of being tremendously alive and sexy and attracted to each other. And then—the whole thing was over. We didn't fight or anything, but there just didn't seem to be much point in it any longer. We still have a kind of special feeling for each other—but it's one of closeness, not of sex.''

Their story runs pretty true to form. Most affairs where sex is the main and only catalyst have a built-in, self-destruct mechanism. The sex act—even for sexual athletes —takes a relatively short time. And then what? The excitement ebbs. The man is rarely as interesting or loving or tender as the woman's own husband and she begins to think more highly of the man at home. There is rarely any future to these relationships. Although divorce is on the increase, I do not believe this is due to extramarital affairs. The root causes of divorce are deeper. And I see no great harm in an affair or even two for the emotionally and sexually mature woman.

As Liz reported, an affair can add a lot to a marriage. That extra sparkle in a woman's eye, that little bounce in her walk, those newly sensuous gestures as she brushes her hair back from her face or shrugs a shoulder, are all tremendous sexual come-ons. Her husband can't help but be intrigued. Even if he doesn't let himself know it on a conscious level (that inner censor again), he knows deep down that someone is finding his wife attractive, sexually attractive. And that stimulates male competitiveness. He starts the courtship all over again. This can turn a dull marriage right around, take the sexual component out of the deep freeze and start the couple off on a more exciting sexual life.

There's another aspect. The woman who has been with her lover all afternoon is hardly in a position to say "no" to her husband at night. Where previously she might have said, "Oh, not tonight," or made some excuse, now guilt renders her ready and welcoming. This pleasant surprise tends to provoke the male to even better performance.

There are other guilt dividends as well that play a positive part in making the marriage better.*

"I found a man who interested me tremendously," another woman told me, "and I interested him. He finds me exciting. I do a lot of daydreaming about him. He fills my thoughts. And instead of feeling guilty, which is the way I suppose I should feel, I feel great. Much better about myself than I used to. My marriage has improved, because I'm taking better care of my husband. I just take better care of everything."

Five years ago I would not have believed that I would ever consider that there could be any justification in the whole wide world for a woman to have an affair. Yet, times have changed and so have I. Where once I would have considered it immoral, unwise and dangerous, I now tend to question these rigid judgments.

There is no getting around the fact that an affair is still considered immoral. But—But what if the affair is good for you? Good for your marriage? Those are big "buts." If an affair strengthens a marriage, then I believe that it may not be completely unwise. It may, in fact, be just what that proverbial doctor ordered to put sparkle and contentment back in a marriage. But like any strong medicine, it can be dangerous. No woman should embark on an affair without thinking of the pitfalls ahead and being sure she can handle them. A woman should ask herself if she is strong enough to keep it to herself, not confide in her friends or leave sly little clues to tantalize her husband. She should be sure she can control her own emotions. And she should

* Note to husbands: If you would prefer that your wife did not take the love affair route to maintain the magic in your marriage, my advice to you is—never stop courting your wife and making her feel that she is the most exciting woman in your world. The woman whose husband is constantly seducing her will never be tempted to stray.

be sure she can keep her lover from intruding into her married life. There should be no mysterious telephone calls or letters that have to be hidden. A lover who insists on driving back and forth past your house will alert your husband to the fact that something is going on. At best, he may think the man is a burglar casing the neighborhood and call the police. At worst, he may start asking you questions. These are just a few of the considerations to ponder before embarking on this risky adventure.

There are affairs that develop into truly meaningful relationships and turn the lives of everyone concerned upside down. When the dust settles, it may prove that everything was for the best—or it may prove to have been a dreadful mistake.

So don't misinterpret what I am saying. I am not giving a blithe go-ahead to the promiscuous wife. I am saying that there are times when the mature woman who is in full control of herself may find an affair not only a pleasure, but something that makes her happier with her marriage. At least that is what increasing numbers of women all over the country are telling me. They are telling me about brief romantic flings with the veterinarian (more women seem to have affairs with vets than with men in other occupations, I don't know why), with old beaux whom they ran into many years later, with the handsome young man who delivered the dry cleaning—and even with the Boy Scout leader. Most of them have been lovely, mad romances that have ended with a gentle tear, a smile and pleasant memories. Men have been having affairs for centuries without endangering their marriages; it seems that now women are availing themselves of the same privilege.

What is sauce for the goose is not prescribed for the gander, however. I am against extramarital affairs for men over 40, not on moral grounds, but because the extra sex can be very dangerous—life-threateningly dangerous. An English pathologist has found that a surprisingly high proportion of male heart attacks occur in the course of extramarital lovemaking. The man, he says, "is tempted into feats of athleticism more in keeping with his younger years. It's a case of striving too hard to please." This physician warns that the man who leads a double life may live only half as long as he might otherwise.

Not all doctors agree. A San Francisco cardiologist says, "If a man dies of a heart attack in a hotel room after intercourse with a prostitute, that fact is likely to be included when the cause of death is determined. But if he dies in bed after intercourse with his wife, it is more likely to be recorded simply that he died in bed."

No matter which doctor you side with, the fact is that most men over 40 don't have that much to go around. Their sexual vigor diminishes. They should save what they have for their wives. (I am convinced that Sam's wife saw very little action from her husband in bed while he was having that affair with Liz. Sam, in his forties, probably cut way down on marital sex during those six months.)

Sometimes it is possible to revitalize one's sex life by as simple an act as giving up smoking. Doctors have discovered that smoking reduces sexual desire and pleasure. Too many cigarettes can prevent a woman from reaching orgasm by numbing cells in the nervous system. If you don't achieve orgasm easily, stop smoking for a few weeks and you'll feel the difference.

There is another vital reason to stop smoking for sex's sake. Smoking lowers your temperature. Nicotine causes the arteries to narrow so the flow of blood to the extremities is diminished. Not only does your overall body temperature drop, but your fingers and toes and a man's penis are colder than the rest of the body. Since a slight rise in body temperature is necessary for both men and women to reach their climax, smokers often don't succeed. Between cold feet and a cold penis, their lovemaking cools down rapidly.

It may be even more important for your husband to stop smoking than for you, since men's ability to have and maintain erections diminishes anyway as the years go by. The man who begins to have difficulty in getting hard becomes more and more nervous and less and less able unless you can help him. One 49-year-old husband (and incidentally a man who had fathered eleven children) put it this way, "Men have varying degrees of sexual worries. Some have anxiety, while others suffer from sheer panic. Anxiety is the first time you can't rise to the requirement for seconds, sexually speaking. And panic is the second time you can't get up for firsts."

The loving, sexually involved woman will never allow her man to develop sexual anxiety, let alone panic out of sheer self-interest. A nonexpectant approach is sometimes all that is needed for a man to recover his sexual bounce. Make bedtime a time for tender cuddling and talk and as he gradually becomes stimulated by your body he will often surprise himself. This is usually an effective prescription.

If it does not work with your man, however, make sure you are not unwittingly turning him off or that he is not putting himself under some kind of pressure that weakens his sexual drive. There are five common danger points in the later years.

1. He may be working too hard, worrying about competition from younger men, putting himself under too much stress. A concerned wife will search for ways of lessening home pressures so he does not have to cope with those on top of office stress. There may be no easy solution to the

overwork problem, but if the two of you talk it over together, and if you point out that too much work results in much too little sex (see footnote on page 148), this may spur him into making some changes.

2. If he suffers from high blood pressure or any other chronic condition, his medication may be lowering his interest in sex to the zero point. His doctor may be able to prescribe an alternative medication without these side effects if the matter is brought to his attention.

3. Overeating and drinking are counter-productive sexwise. A couple of drinks can absolutely block the ability of a man over 50 to have an erection. If he feels he has to drink to get in the mood, try to get him off hard liquor and onto wine. Champagne is supposed to be the wine of romance. You might try a sparkling glass of champagne instead of his usual Scotch on the rocks—and wait and see. Researchers have found that the level of the male sex hormone, testosterone, falls sharply when a man drinks. This probably explains the poor sexual performance of men who drink more than they should—or even have a couple of drinks before making love. Eating may be even more difficult to cope with. Fat men are notoriously bad sexual partners. For the best sex after 45, both men and women should maintain their weight at or under what they weighed—or what they should have weighed—at 25.

4. The depression that some refer to as the male menopause can be debilitating. It is all tied up with men's feelings that they have reached 40 or 45 or 50 and have gone as far as they ever will. They spend a lot of time brooding over this. Some men have to be treated with drugs and therapy. Others snap out of it by themselves. Then there are men who try to prove that they are better than ever by running around with younger women. This may buoy them up for the moment, but when the younger woman

has had enough of the relationship, the man often becomes more depressed than before. Either way it is downright death on his marital sexual relationship.

All things being equal, I would advise a woman who loves her husband to wait it out for a while. If he continues the pattern, then she must get up and about the business of living her own life. But don't be too hasty. This period is like a second adolescence for many men. They just don't know which emotional end is up. The woman who is willing to wait and to try to rebuild her husband's self-confidence may find that this is only a temporary aberration—one that can be forgiven and forgotten as soon as it is passed.

5. Your own warm sexual desires may even be turning your husband off. He may feel threatened by your strong sex urge, just as my actress friend's husband was. Your desires and his capabilities may no longer mesh. And this makes him feel dreadful and weakens his sexual capabilities, sometimes to the vanishing point. Men think of themselves as sexual objects even more than women are thought to. When they find that women have more sexual vigor than they do, it seems to paralyze them. The only solution to this is tender loving care. Don't push him. Don't scare him. Don't make him feel inadequate. Show him plenty of love and affection and his sexual aggression will probably resurface and he will give you multiple orgasms forever after.

The thing to remember is that women are truly fortunate in their sexual life. It gets better as we get older. And yet, if necessary, we can exist happily and healthily without it. Our masturbatory orgasms are really tremendous, as my young friend Claudia discovered. But it is also possible to adjust to less sex, very little sex, or even no sex at all without ill effects. Sexual deprivation does not affect most women seriously. They do not dry up and wither away. They continue whole, warm, hearty and full of vitality, which is more than men can say for themselves. So the rule for women in these second-chance years is—do whatever makes you feel happy and good about yourself.

CHAPTER SIXTEEN

The Myth of Menopause

Not too many years ago, menopause was no myth, but a cruel trick played by nature on women. (Did you know that the female human is the only mammal that experiences the menopause? All other female mammals retain their reproductive abilities until they die.) Where menopause used to signify the end not only of a woman's reproductive life, but often the end of her sex life as well as her vigor and vitality, today it is nothing but a treatable disease. And a rather new disease at that. In 1900, when the life expectancy of the average woman was only 45 years, relatively few women lived to suffer from menopausal problems. But today, when the average woman can look forward to a life span of close to 80 vigorous years, the menopause is a real factor in the life of four-fifths of the female population. The other fifth seems to sail right through this period with absolutely no symptoms, probably because other glands produce enough hormones to compensate for the tapering off and cessation of ovarian production.

But first of all, what *is* the menopause? Startlingly few women really know. This is understandable. After all, menopause was one of the taboo subjects until very recently, along with masturbation, abortion and homosexuality. But no longer.

A simple and brief explanation of the process is given in a remarkable book written by women for women, *Our Bodies, Ourselves.* The following is reprinted from that book with the gracious permission of The Boston Women's Health Book Collective.

"As we get older, our ovaries become less and less able to respond to the ovary-stimulating hormones from our pituitary, which formerly caused the regular maturing and releasing of ova. Since progressively fewer ova are being released, the cyclic production of progesterone is interrupted, and this in turn causes estrogen levels to fall below the amount necessary to start endometrial bleeding (menstruation). The pituitary, without the usual cyclic feedback of estrogen and progesterone, generally overreacts, producing excessive amounts of those hormones that stimulate the ovaries. The result is a hormone imbalance, occurring to different degrees in different women. The most important feature of this hormone imbalance is a decrease in the amount of estrogen to which a woman's system has been accustomed. . . . The symptoms that occur because of the new balance of hormones are chiefly the result of your body's reaction to a drop in estrogen after it has been used to lots of it."

The symptoms vary from woman to woman, and from merely annoying to agonizing. Some are frightening—like the depressions that affect some women; others are downright embarrassing. The hot flashes, for instance. And they are usually totally unnecessary. As I said, menopause is a treatable disease. All too few women are aware of this fact.

I became immediately and personally aware of how ignorant even well-informed women may be when one of my friends told me about her experiences.

"I was determined to get through the menopause on my own," Judy (that's not her real name) said. "I had always believed that the menopause was ninety percent an old wive's tale and ten percent a product of not having enough to do and spending too much time thinking about oneself. Therefore, it should not bother me. I'm very busy and I consider myself emotionally together. I was going to take the menopause in my stride.

"Well, I'm here to tell you that I couldn't. For a while I thought I was going to be one of those women who would not experience it. My forty-ninth birthday came and went. My fiftieth birthday came and went. My fifty-first birthday came—and shortly thereafter, my first hot flash.

"Aha, I said to myself. The menopause. And I thought that this really wasn't too bad. Yes, I was hot and sweaty, but it was just momentary. But that was only the beginning. I learned that the symptoms I had scoffed at before were not in my mind. They were real. I began having hot flashes three or four times a day and then six or seven times a day. I would be sitting at my desk in the office talking to a salesman on the telephone. Hot flashes would be the farthest thing from my mind. And bang. Suddenly a wave of heat would go over me. There would be beads of sweat on my face. Sometimes a trickle of sweat running down my back. I would have to go to the ladies' room and mop myself off with paper towels.

"And at night, too. I could never get comfortable. I would wake up hot and sweaty and throw the covers off. Then I would be cold and clammy. I had three bad colds in two months. I wasn't sleeping well. And neither was my husband. I was so restless I kept waking him.

"Then one day I was offered a new job. I went for an interview. Halfway through, it hit. The sweat was standing out on my face. I didn't know what to do. I thought to myself—if I tell him it's a menopausal hot flash, he'll either think I'm too old or that I'm going to be all emotional and he won't want me. So I said nothing.

"When I got home, I called my gynecologist immediately. I'd had it. My life was not going to be ruled by the menopause. I was no longer going to grit my teeth and tough it out. I wanted my doctor to prescribe some hormones for me.

"But his secretary said he didn't have any free time to see me for the next two weeks unless it was an emergency. When I described my problem, she laughed and said, 'Oh, that's no emergency. You'll still have those in two weeks.'

"When I went to see him two weeks later, he examined me, and afterwards in his office he leaned back in his chair and said, 'Well, I could prescribe hormones for you. We could compensate for the lowered estrogen level that's causing your symptoms, but I'm not going to. They can have dangerous side effects. You're a strong woman. These days you're going to have to use a little extra control. The flashes will pass.'

" 'When?' I asked.

" 'Oh, it's hard to tell,' he said, 'but they shouldn't persist for more than a year or two. Although,' he added cheerfully, 'I have had patients who had flashes for as long as fifteen years.'

" 'Great,' I said. 'And you are not going to do anything for me?'

" 'No,' said Dr. X. 'I'm conservative and I have our best interests at heart. You'll be better off letting nature take her course.'

"*Our* best interests! I thought to myself. What about *my* best interests?"

The next day Judy called me and told me what her doctor had said. I was flamingly indignant. I called her doctor a dinosaur. This is the worst kind of sexism practiced by the medical profession. Many male doctors, either because of a bias against women or because they are unable to understand how menopause affects a woman, feel that the correct thing is to "let nature take its course." If they followed that rule in other diseases, nature would take its course in gallbladder infections, diabetes, tuberculosis, blood poisoning, you name it. This is neither a scientific nor a healing attitude.

I recommended Dr. A., a woman with an absolutely opposite approach. When Judy told her how she had tried to cope with menopausal symptoms by trying to ignore them, Dr. A. shook her head and said sympathetically, "We all get brainwashed, don't we? But there's no reason for you to suffer through this. It is not a sign of weakness to ask for treatment. In fact, if one does not treat the symptoms of menopause, one gives a kind of green light to old age. As far as I am concerned, menopause is not only a treatable disease, but actually a preventable disease.

"When my patients turn forty," Dr. A. went on, "I check estrogen levels just as routinely as I take a Pap smear. When the estrogen level starts going down, I prescribe a supplement to compensate. I tell women to take one pill a day starting on the first of the month and stopping on the twenty-first. This is a rough duplication of the way the ovaries produce estrogen. If necessary, I adjust the prescription from time to time. In this way, a woman need never experience any of the menopause symptoms."

Judy filled her prescription immediately. Her hot flashes continued for another five or six days—and then they disappeared. The next time I saw Judy, she gave me a big hug and said, "I can't thank you enough. Dr. A. has changed my whole life. I didn't know what a state I had let myself get into until my little magic pills got me out of it."

She went on, "You know I had been having a lot of trouble sleeping, partly because of those hot flashes and partly because I just couldn't seem to relax. I had also been doing a lot of worrying, funny little worries, not all of them so little, but the effect was to keep me tense and upset. I was not aware of this until about six weeks after I'd been taking the pills, then one day I suddenly realized how very relaxed and calm I felt. I asked Dr. A. if that had anything to do with taking estrogen and she said, 'Everything.' I feel like a missionary these days. I don't want any other women to have to go through what I did—or think that there is some virtue in suffering through menopause. There isn't. And if their doctor is not sympathetic, I want to tell women to shop around for a more sensitive doctor."

"All right," I said, "I'll use your story in my book. I can't think of a better way to tell women that menopause is a treatable disease and that if they care about themselves, they should have it treated."

One of the least discussed—and most easily treated—symptoms of the menopause is the drying up of vaginal tissues, which makes intercourse quite painful. The lack of lubrication is a direct result of estrogen deprivation. This condition can be reversed promptly by using a hormonal vaginal cream applied with an applicator just the way one inserts a contraceptive cream or jelly.

Women tend to be very reticent about this condition. Some are even too shy to bring it up with their doctors during their checkups. If gynecologists would only make a habit of asking their patients if they have pain during intercourse, it might be easier for women. At any rate, if your vagina is dry and you feel pain instead of pleasure as your lover's penis enters, ask your doctor about this, so that you can start enjoying sex again.

When I talk about menopause, I have to talk about

doctors. As a consequence of being married to a physician, I hear a lot of medical shop talk and I am constantly appalled at how many doctors refer to their older women patients as "crocks." You will never hear them talking this way about a young woman who is sexually attractive to them, no matter how neurotic her symptoms may be, but let a woman reach 45 or 55, and let her start worrying about her menopausal symptoms, and many doctors are bored. She doesn't interest them. They get impatient with her worries. And they joke about these "crocks," with their colleagues. This attitude is changing, but not fast enough. It is common among too many doctors, among too many doctors who are in the field of obstetrics and gynecology. My friend Judy's Dr. X was typical. The fact is that many physicians have not caught up with modern women. They still consider menopause a signal that a woman's meaningful life is at an end. And, even worse, they seem to see no reason for changing this state of affairs. One eminent man was quoted in the prestigious professional journal *Aspects of Human Sexuality* as saying: "Many women fear that they now have lost their main purpose in life and are no longer desired and become seriously depressed. This requires psychiatric intervention."

I would like to suggest to this doctor that he is talking about the women of yesterday. The women of today are more secure. Their identities no longer are dependent solely upon their husbands and children. They are real people. And I suggest that this eminent physician consider treating his patients with hormone therapy rather than shunting them off to the psychiatrist.

Another physician commented, "By the menopausal years the children are grown up and have been or are on the way out of the nest. There is a state of apprehension in the woman. She is suddenly alone once again with the man she married thirty years ago. But he has his nose in *The Wall Street Journal,* and he doesn't look up and say hello to her any more at breakfast, because he is terribly busy making the next move in his career. He is likely to imply again and again, 'Well, now that you and I are stuck with each other, what do we do next?' "

These men I have quoted, physicians though they may be, simply do not understand women. It is as hard for men to adjust to the new freedom women have achieved as it is for them to adjust to the fact that since most women today can expect to live twice as long as women a hundred years ago, medical treatment must change to cope with the challenges of the new female longevity. The menopausal woman is no longer an insecure aging female who has lost her purpose in life. She is a vital, attractive woman who is eagerly looking forward to a whole new lifetime of freedom and opportunity, a lifetime in which she can use the wisdom acquired from forty to fifty years of living, to finally fulfill her potential.

Not all doctors are such stick-in-the-muds. Many are open-minded and eager to maintain a woman's vigor and looks for as long as possible. Many, like Dr. A., believe in treating the menopause as a preventable disease. Hormone therapy is no Fountain of Youth, but it does slow down the aging clock and there is no reason for most women not to take advantage of this. It can mitigate many of the degenerative changes, like the loss of calcium from the bones, that are a consequence of estrogen deprivation. This lack of calcium causes symptoms that mimic arthritis so closely that it is often misdiagnosed. Estrogen replacement also combats loss of muscle tone and substance, another painful degenerative change that may also be misdiagnosed as arthritis. And there are other aging changes that can be postponed, including loss of elasticity in the skin, which means postponing wrinkles. Estrogen also seems to protect women against the heart attacks that may strike after menopause when they no longer enjoy the immunity previously conferred by natural hormone production.

Have you ever noticed how most 60-year-old women look older than their 60-year-old husbands? The reason is that the male does not undergo hormonal deprivation the way the female does. In ten years' time, however, I suspect that a 60-year-old woman will look much younger than her 60-year-old husband because she will have been taking estrogen pills to compensate for mother nature's dirty trick of turning off the ovaries too early.

My husband Milt says, "If a male at any age were to lose his testicular function and were to develop a rounding of his body contours, develop breasts, for instance, and suffer a loss of libido, there is hardly a physician in the world who would hesitate to give him testicular hormones. If someone were to lose his thyroid function and to suffer the metabolic consequences of underactive thyroid, no one would hesitate to give him thyroid. This goes for every other endocrinal gland except the ovary. And because the ovary naturally stops producing hormones, it has been assumed that this is only right and proper. I question this assumption."

So do I. And yet, there are still medical men like Dr. X who pride themselves on refusing to prescribe estrogen for menopausal women. Except for the instances I shall discuss below, there is no reason to deny this aid to women.

Should every menopausal woman take estrogen?

NO. And this is a big NO. First of all, the approximately one-fifth of the female population who experience no menopausal symptoms do not need hormonal therapy. Other glands, such as the adrenals, are obviously producing all the estrogen they need.

And for some women it is absolutely out of the question. Estrogen can be very dangerous. A woman who has had fibroid tumors, for instance, or breast cysts, or a history of cancer should not take it. I cannot underline deeply enough the necessity for having your doctor give you a thorough examination and take a complete medical history before prescribing estrogen. The woman who does take estrogen should be religious about having a twice-yearly checkup with her gynecologist—even if all her life once a year was enough. She should also report any bleeding or breast changes immediately. Hormones are powerful and should be treated with respect.

But for most women, this replacement therapy is the key to vigor and vitality. Some women still worry about sex after menopause, whether it is a natural menopause or a surgically induced one from a hysterectomy. There is no reason to worry. One survey showed that eighty-five percent of the women who had undergone hysterectomies in one large hospital reported no change in their interest in sex or in their ability to have an orgasm. About thirteen percent reported that their sex lives had improved. The other two percent said that intercourse was not as satisfactory as it had been before surgery.

And a psychiatrist, Dr. Daniel Lieberman, professor of psychiatry at Jefferson Medical College, says, "There is no reason for concern that at menopause or after, the woman will lose her desire and enjoyment of sex. Most women will continue the same sexual pattern, and with some women there will be an increase in enjoyment of the sexual act. This may be related to loss of fear of pregnancy. Whatever the cause it is not unusual for a woman to indicate that she is now receiving increased pleasure from sex."

No matter how you look at it, the fact that menopause has become a treatable disease makes it the key to woman's

new freedom. All a woman loses is the ability to reproduce—and if anyone wants to undertake that diaper routine in her fifties and cope with an adolescent in her
sixties, well bless her—she can adopt a baby. But the rest of
us have had it. We're into our second-chance years when
we're better than ever.

CHAPTER SEVENTEEN

Shaping the Future—
Your Own Ten-Year Plan

The woman who wants her second-chance years to be the best of all has to work at shaping her future. Life is full of delightful surprises, but you can't just sit back and wait to be surprised. All that is likely to happen to the woman who spends her days in front of the television set is that the ceiling might fall on her.

Most big business corporations have ten-year plans. They look ahead, form "think tank" committees and draw up projections of where the company should be in ten years' time. Women can profit from the same kind of advance planning. Even if you depart from the route you map out, just the fact of having a plan provides a sound base for informed decisions as you go along. It enables you to ask yourself, "Do I really prefer this new direction to the one I chose previously? What are the advantages of making this change? The disadvantages?"

At the very beginning of my career I faced a crucial decision: Did I want the purely academic life of teaching and research that I had been preparing myself for during four years of college and six of graduate school—or did I want to take a chance on the unconventional career that seemed to be opening up after I won "instant fame" as the blond female psychologist whose knowledge of the sport of boxing made her a winner of *The $64,000 Question*. I won more than that $64,000. I won all kinds of opportunities. I had received several radio and television offers. Invitations to write and to lecture had been coming my way. It was all very tempting. If I chose the first fork, I would be teaching, working on laboratory experiments and publishing my research findings in professional journals for my colleagues. If I took this new fork, I would have to give up the research, the teaching and the scholarly reports, but I could study the work of others and explain the most significant new discoveries to the public as a kind of psychological journalist. It would be a kind of teaching, although not on the college or university level. I decided I would prefer to be out in the world involved with people rather than tucked away in some laboratory trying to discover the frustration level of a white rat or if gentlemen really did prefer blondes. I have never regretted the decision.

As we get older, it is more important than ever to plan ahead. These second-chance years are too precious to leave to chance. My diet and exercise regime was part of planning ahead. Not only did I realize that I had let myself go and if I didn't get myself in shape now, it would be much harder to do it in my fifties, but I also knew that if I put on any more weight I might not be considered for future television shows. But whether a woman is in the public eye or not, the importance of starting the second-chance years in optimum physical condition can hardly be overestimated for both physical and emotional health.

This is also the time for a woman to think ahead financially and emotionally, to think carefully about all the people who are important in her life at the moment. Try to envisage what the people who mean most to you today will be doing in the next decade. What do you want your relationship with them to be in ten years?

I have done a lot of thinking about my next ten years, and some of it has already begun to pay off. In ten years, I thought, our daughter Lisa will be graduated from medical school. She will probably be married. She may have a child. Or two. Our present New York City apartment is just not big enough for Lisa and our future son-in-law and our future grandchildren to visit us comfortably. I wanted a place where there would be plenty of room for all of us, a place where the children would have room to play and have fun, where Lisa and her husband could have some privacy; a place they would look forward to visiting.

Then I thought about my parents. Both are still practicing law, but eventually they may decide to retire. If so, it would be lovely if Milt and I had a place that was big enough so they could live with us and at the same time preserve their independence.

Finally I thought about Milt and myself. Our marriage now was better than it had ever been. It was sexually exciting, emotionally rewarding—and cozy. We had discovered a new interest in doing things together. For many years, we had busily pursued our own careers and neither of us would have had it any different. We found great satisfaction in our work—and even greater satisfaction in sharing our experiences with each other. But now we both wanted to do more together, not just report to each other on evenings and weekends what we had been doing.

Yes, I thought to myself. The answer was obvious. We needed a larger apartment. Much larger. Possibly a house.

Then suddenly everything crystallized.

One lazy Sunday morning, Milt said, "Listen to this!" He was excited. He read an ad in the real estate section that sounded like a millionaire's dream—a big house with six bedrooms, a three-car garage, with a small apartment over it, a swimming pool and a tennis court. And it was only an hour's drive from the city. Could we afford it? Probably not. But we decided to look at it anyway. "You know," said Milt, "it might be the answer to my problem."

"Your problem?" I asked. I was mystified. What problem did he have?

"Well, I'm not going to be able to play squash forever," he said. "It is a very tough game. I'm already beginning to feel it in my legs. I've been thinking to myself lately that I ought to move into tennis. You can play that until you're ninety."

So Milt had been making his own ten-year plan, too.

In the "flesh," this millionaire's dream house was nowhere near as charming or palatial as the advertisement had led us to think—and it was much too expensive. But now we knew what we wanted. We wanted a house in the country. A place to go for weekends and summers now. A place to retire to eventually. A place for our future grandchildren to come visit. A place for my folks to live if they ever decided to retire. A place where Milt and I would be learning a thousand new things together. A place for us to swim and play tennis.

It was truly a great idea. Yet if I had not been seriously planning for the next ten years and realized that we needed a larger place, I wonder whether I would have fallen in with the idea of going to look at that first house so enthusiastically. After all, I have always lived in the city. I never wanted to live anyplace else. Even when Lisa was old enough to go to school and we had serious talks about whether we should move to the suburbs for her sake, I was the one who said no.

But now things had changed. Milt's interests and needs had changed. And so had mine. A house in the country now sounded very appealing to this city mouse. It took months to find what we wanted. And the minute we set eyes on it, we knew it was for us. An old farmhouse set on 125 acres. It came complete with barns and sheds and a tenant house, which will be just right for my folks once we get it fixed up. The ad had said it "needed work." And did it ever. It needed heating and plumbing and a new roof and a kitchen. It was a very needy house. We loved it.

Now our lives have a new focus. My idea of a wonderful weekend used to be sleeping late and not getting dressed until it was time to go to the movies or whatever we had planned for Saturday night. These days, I am up early on Saturday morning working in our new vegetable garden, scraping floorboards, painting shutters—and loving it. We made a solemn pact that we would do as much of the work as possible ourselves and that there would be no such thing as men's work and women's work. We share and share alike. And we are learning by doing. We have a new family joke that we are the two best one-armed workers in town. One-armed, because we always have a how-to book in one hand while we are painting or hammering with the other.

Now on weekend evenings, we sit exhausted in our rockers on the old front porch when it's warm or in front of the wood stove in the kitchen when it's cold, and dream about how the place will look one of these days. Some day we will put in that swimming pool. And a tennis court. After we have put in a decent bathroom. After we have put in a new furnace. After we get storm windows. Some day . . . but right now, we sit and dream. We talk about where the pool should go. Over there with a view of the Connecticut hills? Over there where we can turn the tumble-down shed into a pool house? One of these days we will decide, but for now it is tremendously satisfying just to sit and plan at the end of a hard working day.

The farm has put another new spark into our marriage. It is like being off on a fresh adventure. In marriage, just as in business, it is important to look ahead and make sure that there is enough fresh input to ensure that the relationship remains a going concern. Couples need emotional and mental stimulation in regular doses to keep from taking the marriage for granted.

Planning ahead also means making decisions about what you *don't* want to do. I have decided I don't want to sit through any more boring evenings at the opera or the ballet. They are wasted on me. Why should I take up a seat that someone who really loves opera could use? I have cut way down on meaningless entertaining. We had become caught up in the business of the X's asking us for dinner and our returning the invitation and their asking us back again. This pattern had become established with several couples. Now I feel free to refuse invitations. And I no longer ask people over because we "owe" an invitation; no, we ask people over when we really want to see them. I stopped the radio program that I had done for six years in New York. It was becoming repetitive and I had learned all I could from it.

Cutting out unrewarding and boring activities has given me time to take on new interests. When I heard that the dramatic rights for a book I had enjoyed enormously were available, for instance, I snapped them up. Now a screen treatment is being prepared and I am looking for backing. It is a whole new fascinating world.

I have other, more ambitious projects that I want to start work on in the next decade. The time is going to come when I won't want to jet all over the country to give lectures and appear on television. I have been doing that for a long time. Today I am much more interested in serving people directly and soon I am going to try to carve out a second career for myself—in politics this time.

My dream is to be a United States senator from the State of New York. I believe in aiming high. While I know that I will have to start on the local level and may never reach the Senate, I prefer to pin my hopes to a star rather than to the lowest branch of the smallest tree. There is no point in my saying, "If I can just get elected dog catcher, I'll be happy." I won't be.

Whatever one wants to do in the second-chance years, whether it is to run for senator, get married, go to China, start your own business, this is the time to take the first step. And the first step is to make a plan. Think ahead. Where do you want to be in ten years? What do you want to be doing? How do you want people to respond to you? What relationship do you want to have with the people who are important to you today ten years from now? What about if someone you love dies in the next ten years? (This has to be faced.) How do you want to live? And where?

It is a good idea to write down your answers to these questions—and then keep thinking about them over a period of several weeks. Pull out your answer sheet every few days and review it. As you consider your future in depth, your answers will evolve into more thoughtful and detailed guidelines.

Then, when you think that you have considered all aspects of the direction you want your life to take in the next decade, ask yourself the ultimate question, "What do I really want out of the rest of my life?" Sigmund Freud, in an exasperated mood, once asked, "My God, what do these women want?" The answer to that is very simple. I'm surprised he had to ask. Most women want a chance to fulfill their potential. And that is what the second-chance years offer—thirty or forty more years to live the life you want to live.

In the next chapter I will tell you how five women, one of them my sister, worked to shape their futures and fulfill their potential.

CHAPTER EIGHTEEN

Achieving the Perfect Future

Today there is such pressure on women to get up and out of the house and into an office or profession that the woman who truly enjoys making a home feels guilty, or even retarded. I find this very distressing. Some women are blissfully happy once they get out of the house and are working at no matter what; other women's bliss is centered in the home. And there is nothing wrong with either way.

There are hundreds of thousands of women who find the life of a housewife absolutely satisfying. Even when their children are grown, they find fulfillment in the lives they have constructed with loving care and grace around the home and hearth. The backbone of their communities, they work for better schools, a cleaner environment, more responsible government. They supply the warmth and the continuity that is the glue holding society together.

Should these women go out and get paying jobs? Not unless they want to. Or have to. Some women have no choice in the matter. The unmarried woman must support herself. The divorcee and the widow, even though they might prefer to stay at home, may be forced into the nine-to-five working world. If so, they should not waste time feeling sorry for themselves. The single woman is generally better off in the working world; it offers more stimulus than life alone at home. And if a woman wants to remarry, she is hardly likely to trip over a prospective husband between the kitchen sink and the stove.

Almost every woman over 40 has the opportunity to shape her future to her liking—although some do not recognize that opportunity. My friend Marcia, for instance. With one child married, one in college and the other in high school, the time had come when she had freedom to do almost anything she wanted to. But she didn't know what she wanted.

"I like my life," she said. "I've tried to plan ahead, and you know what I want to do in the next ten years? Exactly what I'm doing now. Except—," and she paused, "I'm bored. And I don't know why. My life suits me to a T. Except that I'm too fat. I hate the way I look."

"Get out of the house," I told her. "The minute you get some of that weight off, you'll feel better about yourself. And you'll look better. The thing to do is get out and keep yourself busy so you won't be snacking in the kitchen all the time."

"It's easy to say, 'get out of the house,'" Marcia complained. "What do I do once I get out?"

She is an old friend, so I let myself get the tiniest bit exasperated. "Oh, for heaven's sakes," I told her. "Go for a walk. Jog for a mile. Stand on your head. Go to a movie. Call on someone. Do something.

"Look," I told her, "if you can't think of anything you want to do, go for a long walk every day. Three miles at a minimum; five miles would be better. Think about what you see, whom you meet. Think about the weather. Think about the part of your walk you like most. And if, when you get home, you haven't seen anything that appealed to you, at least you were out of the house getting fresh air and exercise. And the next day, walk in a different direction."

"Okay," Marcia grumbled, "but all that will probably happen to me is that I'll get run over."

She did not get run over, of course. She telephoned me a few weeks later and said, "I have to hand it to you. You knew what you were talking about.

"One day as I was going out for my hike—and incidentally I've lost weight—a neighbor pulled alongside me and said she was going in town to the flower show. Would I like to come. Of course I would, although I'd never been to a flower show in my life. It was a revelation. I came home with three potted plants under my arm and packets and packets of seeds. I'm fascinated. I've bought some books on houseplants. Last week I went to our local nursery and asked if they would let me help out in the greenhouses for free so that I could learn. They agreed and I go every morning from 8:30 to 12:00."

"Well, that's better than getting run over," I teased her.

"Yes," she said, "you know, I just couldn't believe that something as simple as going for a walk could lead to anything."

But it can. You never know what is going to open the door onto something wonderful. But you have to get out where the doors are. Very little that is wonderful is going to happen to you if you don't meet it halfway.

Even women like Marcia whose lives are centered around the home need stimulation and fresh interests if they are to continue to grow, to have meaningful lives and to keep that light in their eyes that comes from having something of their own. It is even more important for the woman at home to work at expanding her horizons, because too often she is isolated from new ideas and new people by the very facts of suburban geography.

My sister Elaine was just the opposite. By the time her oldest child was in college, she knew that she wanted to get out of the house and play a meaningful part in the world. She had always been absorbed in our parents' law work and would question our Dad for hours on end about this case and that legal point. She decided she, too, was going to be a lawyer.

Elaine did it the hard way. She went to law school nights. It took six years for her to earn her degree. And all the time she kept up with her housework and the children. Although the children really did their part. As soon as they realized that their mother was not faithful Fido any more who would fetch and carry for them, they were very cooperative about taking on more responsibility. And her husband was gracefully understanding about Elaine tearing out of the house every night to go to class.

She was obviously a born lawyer. She passed the bar exam the first time around, something very few law aspirants manage to do, and she was immediately offered a clerkship to a judge. A year later, she decided to open her own law office.

She had some misgivings, but our folks encouraged her. "All you need is a sign on the door, a secretary and a typewriter," my mother said. So Elaine went ahead. She had a coffee for all the women in her neighborhood and told them her plans. Soon she began to have a number of clients. Many women had small problems that they felt a male lawyer would be impatient with or not consider worth his time. They brought them all to Elaine.

The next thing that happened was that she was asked to teach. And the university gave her a professorship immediately. Now, only ten years after she enrolled in law school, she has been appointed to a state office in New Jersey. I haven't dared ask my sister Elaine what her plans are for the next ten years. I'm scared she'll want to run for senator, too.

The changes in my sister are fantastic. She looks better and younger than she did ten years ago. She has lost weight. She dresses better. And she carries herself with a kind of swing that she never had before. As a sister, I can say it. She has become a very attractive woman. When I told her this, she smiled and said, "That's nice. I know I'm more interesting these days. I used to have absolutely nothing to say to people. I'd be off in a corner with the other wives swapping recipes. Today I'm in the center of a group when I go to parties with people asking me what I think about a state income tax or busing. I don't know why I wasted so much time before."

She stopped and thought a moment then said, "Oh, I know why. And it wasn't wasted time. It was three children and well worth it. If I had it all to do over again, I'd do it the same way."

Elinor, a divorcee I met during a lecture tour, took my words about making a ten-year plan to heart. Her ten-year plan included a short-term goal of losing 15 pounds, a longer-term goal of earning enough money to send her children to college, and a long-term goal of becoming an executive.

"I almost didn't care executive of what," she told me. "I just knew that after twenty years of running my own household and being Queen Bee that I wouldn't be happy in a job where I wasn't the boss. I didn't think I'd learn how to take orders gracefully."

Elinor decided that selling was her best avenue toward an executive position. She had always been the one who collected the most for the Community Chest, who sold the most ads for the PTA program, who organized the Girl Scout cookie drives. Her first job was in a department store. The pay was terrible and the commissions almost invisible. Then one night she was sitting home with her shoes off and feet up trying to figure out which bills she had to pay and which could be put off until next month. The insurance premium was one of the "musts." This made her stop and think. "I'd never seen a woman selling insurance," she told me. "And that's ridiculous. Women are just as concerned about insurance as men—even more so. And a woman understands better than a man what it means to be alone and have children to care for. I suddenly shivered, wondering what would happen to my 16-year-old Jenny and 14-year-old Bill if I got run over. It dawned on me that I really needed insurance to provide for my children. Sure, my ex-husband had some, but I couldn't depend on that. And no one had come around selling insurance to me. When I was married, insurance brokers were always sending my husband letters asking if he had sufficient coverage. But I, when I really needed it, didn't get as much as a telephone call."

Elinor wrote a dozen letters to insurance companies asking for a job. She finally landed one with an insurance broker who dealt with many companies.

"I haven't looked back since," she says. "Now I specialize in helping women get the insurance coverage they need. It is a brand-new field—and a very profitable one. I'm not the top executive I dreamed of being, but I am my own boss more or less. And that's good enough for me."

Another woman I greatly admire is a widow. She has had a routine job in publicity that she had held all her married life. It was fun, although not financially very rewarding.

When her husband died at a brutally young 50, it turned out that he had left practically no insurance. She and the children had to cut their scale of living way down. This loss of security plus the loss of her husband threw her into an emotional tailspin for months. She nearly had a nervous breakdown. As a way of working out her problems and feelings, she began writing about them. Her scribbled notes, often written in the middle of the night when she could not sleep, turned out to be the beginning of a book. Eventually she produced a book which was of great help to many bereaved women. Soon, she was receiving requests to lecture about widowhood and bereavement. Today, she has a whole second career of lecturing and counseling widows on how to cope with their grief and make new lives for themselves.

The woman who does not have to concern herself primarily with money starts off with more options when it comes to shaping her future. But all the same, it takes planning.

Phyllis, the wife of one of Milt's colleagues, decided at 42 that it was time she got back into the working world. Her previous experience had been very limited. She had been a girl Friday in an advertising agency for a year before she got married. This was enough for her to know that she did not want to go into advertising. She decided that she would feel more at home in something to do with books or magazines or journalism. Even this broad a goal was enough to cut out, for instance, real estate, teaching, computer programing and hundreds of other fields.

"But what can I do?" she asked me. "I've been at home with the children all these years. What could I possibly contribute to any of these fields?"

I suggested she find out by going to one of the employment agencies that specialize in supplying temporary help. This is an excellent way to see any number of different businesses from the inside, to meet new people, to polish up old skills and acquire new ones. It also helps the married woman make the transition from home to office life at her own pace. It is not easy to shift one's life-style even if it is a shift a woman wants to make. There is a great deal of stress involved. The woman who works as a "temporary" has the option of spacing her jobs so that she can get into the swing of business life gradually.

Phyllis had no skills except typing. And that was rather impressionistic. The agency found her a job at a medical magazine to fill in while the receptionist was on vacation. After that, she filled in as a receptionist at a radio station. She had eight receptionist jobs in six months.

Then, by one of those really odd coincidences, she got her "dream job" while she was working for her husband. His receptionist had gone on vacation and he suggested that since she was working for other people, she might help him out for three weeks. One day a patient looked at her in a rather perplexed way and said, "I'm sorry. I'm sure I know you from somewhere, but I can't remember where." He was the editor of the medical magazine where she had had her first job.

Phyllis laughed. "I was your receptionist six months ago," she said. She told him about her plan to get back into the business world and how she wanted to work on a magazine or a newspaper or in some allied field.

"Why don't you come work for us?" the man asked. "We have an opening for a researcher. It's more interesting than being a receptionist and other things may open up. Since your husband is a physician, you are probably somewhat familiar with the field. Why don't you think about it?"

She didn't have to think long. As soon as her husband's receptionist was back from vacation, Phyllis went right downtown to work on the magazine.

She now does some writing and reporting on medical

findings and thoroughly enjoys her job. It wasn't quite what she had aimed for, but close enough. And she feels very good about herself, when her husband's colleagues ask her about new breakthroughs in medicine that the magazine had reported on. "They never used to really look at me," she said. "You know how it is, at dinner parties those doctors all get in a corner and talk shop and leave the women to gossip. Now I talk shop, too."

All five of these women, all of them over 40, made fresh starts in life—some through choice, some through necessity —and all of them are living happier lives than before. Even the widow says, "Just the fact of being forced to get out into the world and work seriously, not just play at working, has made me realize that up until now I had never lived anywhere near to my potential. I am a person of much more status today. I don't know whether that is necessarily good. But it isn't bad. I feel that it is right, that people should make the most of themselves. What is wonderful is that today being forty-five doesn't hold you back."

And it doesn't. The years after 40 are truly the butterfly years of happiness. But remember, happiness is nothing you can go out looking for. It is a by-product of involvement and commitment. You can never say, "I'm going to make myself happy." It just does not work that way. But if you are going about your life's work of using all your abilities to the utmost, one day when you are in the middle of something—hanging the laundry outside on a sunny day, negotiating a contract, making love, starting intermediate Chinese in your second year back at college, baking bread—you will suddenly become aware that you feel good. In fact, you feel great. In fact, you feel *happy!*

The only way to achieve that feeling is to say, "I'm going to spend my days doing the things I do best and like best and I'm really going to get involved." And then, some day, when you are not expecting it, you will wake up and say, "I am a happy woman."

That is what the second-chance years are all about. A chance to reach to the limits of your potential, a chance to live happily ever after.